Tokyo Tempos

Tokyo Tempos

By Michael Pronko

Copyright © 2024 Michael Pronko

First English Edition, Raked Gravel Press

All rights reserved worldwide. This book may not be reproduced in any form, in whole or in part, without written permission from the author.

Interior Design by BEAUTeBOOK www.beautebook.comn

Cover © 2024 Andy Bridge www.andybridge.com

ALSO AVAILABLE BY MICHAEL PRONKO

Memoirs on Tokyo Life
Beauty and Chaos: Slices and Morsels of Tokyo Life (2014)
Tokyo's Mystery Deepens: Essays on Tokyo (2014)
Motions and Moments: More Essays on Tokyo (2015)

The Detective Hiroshi Series
The Last Train (2017)
The Moving Blade (2018)
Tokyo Traffic (2020)
Tokyo Zangyo (2021)
Azabu Getaway (2022)
Shitamachi Scam (2023)

TOKYO TEMPOS

by Michael Pronko

Raked Gravel Press 2023

Contents

PREFACE 13

PART ONE LIVING HERE 21

    INTRODUCTION 23
    TRAIN TIME 25
    CAN YOU SEE FUJI FROM THERE? 31
    TWO BOYS ON THE TRAIN 37
    MORE THAN SENDING A LETTER 41
    TOKYO OPEN AND CLOSED 47
    PHOTOGRAPH EVERYTHING 53
    NEXT DOOR CLOSE 59
    ADVICE IN TOKYO 65

PART TWO SEASONS AND RITUALS 69

    INTRODUCTION 71
    MISSING MEISHI 73
    BEAUTY BLOSSOMING 79
    BLOSSOMS AND STONE 85
    THE NEW YEAR OF APRIL AND MAY 89
    SUMMER'S DIVIDE 95
    SUDDEN FIREWORKS 101
    TOKYO CHRISTMAS TREES 107
    A CLEAN ENDING 113
    108 BELLS 119

PART III SMALL INTENSITIES 123

    INTRODUCTION 125

    A Procession of Pottery 127
    Tokyo Masked.. 133
    Breaking Homes... 137
    Tatami Change... 143
    Bone *Sake* 149
    Tokyo Arrows 153
    Tokyo Toads 157
    Ramen Everywhere 163

PART FOUR TEACHING IN TOKYO 169

    Introduction 171
    Turnabout is Fair Play—Wedding Speeches..................... 173
    Outside the Classroom 181
    Rights in the Matter 189
    Context for My Outrage 197
    Tears for English 205
    Before I Taught a Poem I'd Ask to Know.......................... 213
    Surgery and Cranes 221

GLOSSARY.. 229

THANKS 233

ABOUT THE AUTHOR... 235

"Rome was a poem pressed into service as a city."
— Anatole Broyard

* * *

"We don't see the world as it is. We see it as we are."
— Anais Nin

* * *

"Tokyo. You hear about it. You go see it.
And a window opens up into a whole new thing. And you think: What does this mean? What do I have left to say? What do I do now?"
— Anatole Broyard

Preface

Writing Finds Me

One evening

One evening years ago, after a drinking party with students, I was heading through Shinjuku Station with one of my students who took the same train line. Suddenly, I took her arm and shuffled out of the rush of people. I pulled my pen and notebook from my pocket to scribble down an idea that had just clicked.

She was an aspiring journalist (and later become one, and a teacher too), but she was then perhaps not used to people stopping in the swirl of the world's busiest station. We were just two of the 3.6 million passengers that pass through the station every day. She waited patiently, though, as Japanese students are trained to do, until I was done scribbling my notes. "An essay found me, and I didn't want it to escape," I sheepishly explained.

She looked at me and laughed. "Sensei, does that happen all the time?" "Just at odd times," I said. "But you have to get it down before it disappears."

If I were a quicker-thinking teacher, I would have quoted Francis Bacon: "Write down the thoughts of the moment. Those that come unsought for are commonly the most valuable." I learned that the hard way—write it down, or it'll disappear.

About ten years ago, I eased out of a decade-plus of writing for Newsweek Japan, The Japan Times, and other publications and switched my focus to novels. Since then,

I've written one novel a year, with an annual word count not so different from those busy years. Still, it was a nice change of canvas size.

The novels in the Detective Hiroshi series drew heavily on what I'd written about in those earlier pieces. And though I like the characters in my stories, I've missed writing directly in my own voice. When do I get to say what *I* think? When is it *my* turn? This book is my turn. It's what didn't disappear.

Tokyo's vastness

I don't think anyone could claim to know Tokyo completely. This is the fifth book I've written about Tokyo life, and I don't think I've captured even a small portion of it. But that's OK. Being complete is one thing; being interesting is another. Even after twenty-plus years, I find the city a fascinating place to live, write, and think.

In that sense, this is a guide into and an account of my journey through Tokyo. But it's not exactly a travel book; it's more about how my heart and mind respond to Tokyo life as I wander, work, and live here every day.

If you want a history of Tokyo, there are plenty of those. I love reading them. And if you want explanations and analyses, to be "assured of certain certainties," as T.S. Eliot wrote, you can find those too. You can climb to the top of too-tall buildings for a panoramic view of the vastness, but those spots leave you distant from what's happening. But I want to write close to life. It's there that I find the most interesting and meaningful insights.

In the train system in the Tokyo metropolitan area, there are always multiple ways to get from one place to another—faster ways, cheaper routes, easier transfers, longer waits, and nicer walks. You have to choose. These writings are my choice of routes for the journeys through the heart of Tokyo. It's not that I saw Tokyo completely. It's that I tried to experience it fully.

Seeing Tokyo

Henry David Thoreau said, "It's not what you look at that matters; it's what you see." That's definitely true in Tokyo, where looking is unavoidable, but seeing takes effort. As the Zen Buddhists say, a finger pointing at the moon is not the moon. Words pointing at Tokyo are not Tokyo, granted. But words can point in directions that reveal life's delightful and intriguing parts. Words are a way to see inside Tokyo.

Tokyo resists neat summations. Its contradictions refuse resolution. Tokyo is known for its centrifugal energies as much as its cleanliness and order. But I like that inability to see everything. Taking it in pieces is fine. Sharing snippets and vignettes is a large part of the urban experience.

I'm writing to people who have visited, have lived here, or will visit or live here, and maybe want to think more about the city. But I also want to share Tokyo with those who might say, "I would never live in a place like that." Readers are always armchair travelers in some sense, so wherever you are, enjoy the reading, thinking, or rethinking, wherever you may be.

Over the years

The first three books in the Tokyo Moments series, *Beauty and Chaos*, *Tokyo's Mystery Deepens*, and *Motions and Moments*, won awards and good reviews for their personal and offbeat approach to Tokyo. Since 2015, when the last book in this series was published, millions of tourists have poured through Japan; the reader might even be one of them. The photos and videos posted of Japan multiply constantly. So why not just take more pictures? I could do that.

So, is this book better than Instagram? That's hard to say. I like visuals, but I like language too. Instagram elevates marvelous shots of slivers of the world that you might never otherwise see. Writing articulates ideas and thoughts about slivers of the world in ways you might not think of. I think both are valuable. The writings in this volume are snapshots of my experience, but words explore the ideas that flow from those experiences.

Most visitors flying into Japan were probably introduced to the country through movies or manga. Those visual story forms are one way to reflect on life in Japan, but there are others. Whether fiction or nonfiction, novels, old or new films, manga or anime, there is a massive literary and cultural reflection on Tokyo life. That's maybe as it should be. Richness produces richness.

Living in Tokyo for a large chunk of my life, I feel that richness every day. "Everything I see or hear is an essay in bud. The world is everywhere whispering essays," said Alexander Smith, essay writer and theorist. In Tokyo, that whisper is often multiple whispers at the same time. Which bud should be plucked first? Images work their magic, and words work theirs.

Writing Tokyo

The first third of my life was singularly American. Since then, I suppose I've been transnational, traveling and living in different countries, usually in densely urban spaces. I like nature and the countryside just as much as the city, but

Tokyo is where I'm writing from, what I write about, and what shapes my view. It's been that way for a while.

Wherever I was, traveling the world, teaching in Beijing, and studying in the States, inner compulsion kept me writing. And then, in Tokyo, I got some lucky breaks. When I settled in Tokyo, I wrote for a start-up online magazine called Tokyo Q. From there, I got invited to write a column for Newsweek Japan. That column ran from 2003 to 2014. A small publisher gathered my columns into book form in Japanese—three times. Then, I put them into English as the Tokyo Moments series.

I also wrote about art and architecture for *Artscape Japan* and did a few TV shows based on my essays for *NHK* and *Nihon Television*. I wrote about jazz for a magazine in Italy, for *Blue Note Japan*, and helped found a bilingual print magazine called *Jazznin*. I wrote about music for *The Japan Times* and took on whatever writing opportunities arrived in my inbox. And did I mention my day job at a university teaching literature?

Then the overload of deadlines finally pushed me to take a break from short-form writing. The weekly task of pulling together a set of ideas about serious topics was constant and intense. Christmas and New Year and personal vacations were no exception. Newspapers and magazines don't have holidays. The experience of writing to weekly deadlines was a lesson in discipline, dedication, concision, and compression. It was a period of breathing out without enough breathing in. I've finally caught my breath.

I kept the jazz writing, though. You can see that on my website, Jazz in Japan. Jazz has remained a refuge and an infusion of creativity for me. It's the hardest thing to write about in some ways, as words always fail to capture the music, but it keeps me working on finding the right words.

Writing the novels in the Detective Hiroshi series reminded me that novels can contain almost anything—real places, fake places, conversations, descriptions, arguments, historicizing, and editorializing. Novels run on both logical patterns and emotional pressures. However, essays have a self-contained focus that is more personal and revealing, intimate and confessional, and unresolved. I like both.

And you may ask yourself…
Meanwhile, Tokyo keeps updating itself, tearing down buildings, opening new train stations, building new train lines, leaving some good things behind, and finding new ones. There's little sense of impending doom or economic collapse here. Of course, it's lurking behind the rushing around. The pandemic bankrupted many stores, bars, and restaurants but dropped rents so new ones could start. Somehow, Tokyo keeps repairing its small parts as the whole keeps moving forward.

When I wrote about Tokyo in novel form, the city often served as the setting. But in these essays, I bring Tokyo out of the background to see it for what it is. I want to ground myself in the city's sense-seducing power and consider, as in the Talking Heads song "Once in a Lifetime," "Well, how did I get here?" As a philosophy major in Tokyo, that question comes up often.

Thoughts and insights have their own duration and scope, like a prayer or confession. I let some of the essays in this collection find their own length but kept each one short enough to finish in the time it takes to go from one express train station to the next. I don't want to bury the zing of curiosity in wordiness, but I don't want to force the brevity, either. I don't have a grand, unified theory of Tokyo, but I do have observations and insights.

The writing is rooted in decades of living here, trying to see without giving up the pleasure of looking. I've chosen topics that I think go to the heart of life here. Many of the essays emerge from aspects of Tokyo that the casual visitor or the busy-minded resident might not notice. Some meander, while others head right to the point. Some are contemplative rather than argumentative. Others wonder without the need to conclude. That fits Tokyo, which seems different every day.

Arthur Benson, in a 1922 essay called "The Art of The Essayist," said: "It will be seen, then, that the essay need not concern itself with anything definite; it need not have an intellectual or a philosophical or a religious or a humorous motif; but equally none of these subjects are ruled out. The only thing necessary is that the thing or the thought should be vividly apprehended, enjoyed, felt to be beautiful, and expressed with a certain gusto."

Gusto. That's what these writings strive for—a delight in Tokyo's enigmas, an embrace of Tokyo's often-hidden nature, and a comfort with the intensity and complexity of the place. Enjoy!

Part One
Living Here

Introduction

Over the past few decades, I've probably stopped noticing as many things as I've started noticing. As time passes, the freshness of certain experiences washes away. The mind sees the same things, accepts them as normal, and stops thinking about them. I always hate losing that sense of fresh shock and off-balance confusion about life here, but there might be no better way to survive the onslaught of sensory input. If you don't look too much, you can save a lot of energy. If you look too closely, the city can drain you and send your mind whirring. I try to find a balance.

Most quintessential Tokyo experiences seem "normal" to me now, but many of those essentials are always at risk of losing their normalness and becoming unfamiliar again. I'm not sure how or why certain experiences that have become part of living in Tokyo suddenly strike me as unique, questionable, engaging, and deserving of being written about. But they do.

The critic and theorist Victor Shklovsky had this to say about the normalizing of life and what response we might make to it: "Habitualization devours objects, clothes, furniture, one's wife, and the fear of war. If all the complex lives of many people go on unconsciously, then such lives are as if they had never been. Art exists to help us recover the sensation of life; it exists to make us feel things." I couldn't agree more.

Responding to the world keeps them from disappearing—not from existing in any physical sense, of course. The world remains. But things can quickly lose their intrigue and meaning. When that happens, we lose any clear way toward understanding them. The topics in this section are drawn from everyday experiences and situations, but ones that I feared could quickly slip down the drain of "Oh, that. Well, of course."

There's a lot of danger in "of course." It's the danger of losing the vitality in the world and our reaction to it. Ironically, the longer things persist in our lives, the weaker meanings they offer. But they can be excavated, dusted off, set before us, and reconsidered. In this section, "Living Here," I want to re-consider these everyday experiences to rediscover the meanings I found and still find before they get lost forever. If you notice a sense of desperation or urgency here, I suppose there is one.

Train Time

The doors shut with a familiar whoosh, everyone balances themselves, settles in, then the motion, too subtle to notice at first, begins. There is a floating sensation, my feet lifting, my mind lifting, the city falling away on both sides.

Some people find Tokyo's trains an annoyance. The Chuo Line—"my" train—is crowded and often late. Other people may use their train time to snooze, text, shop, game, or watch some sports/drama/film unfold on a hand-size screen. For me, train time is meditative.

I reflect on the day ahead or the day done, on the people in gentle motion, the passing stations, the city beyond. I like the train's lulling sound as I'm moved around the city, wrapped in sensations, taken away from all the stuff I have to do, and put close to people I don't have to know.

I'm not sure if, like Walt Whitman, I contain multitudes, but Tokyo trains definitely do. I think of other passengers as a mantra of lives not lived. It's unsettling to consider all the paths not taken, all the stations unvisited, the areas left untrod. But it's a good unsettling. I like the human hive of a Tokyo train, watching the social dance around me, sensing the meanings in small actions, being drawn in by the magnetism of human complexities.

At times, I feel discomfited by the density of the human possibilities spread out before me. The panoply of people is a recitation of life's vast choices. There are hundreds of people on a single train who live other lives, do other things, think other thoughts. My train ride includes an exhibit of lives I'll never see more than a few minutes of. It's not speed dating; it's speed observation.

It's just as Joni Mitchell sings in *Hejira*, "I see something of myself in everyone." Watching people in various states of sleepiness, I position myself on the continuum of fatigue. Seeing their clothes, I can tell what they're doing that day. From the wrinkles in their brows, I sense their day's pressures and compare them to mine. Of course, they're observing everyone else too, only they do it more discreetly. Train time is the last mirror before job, school, or meeting significant others.

Salarymen, students, retirees, and workers tend to follow their assigned forms, but their inner lives go unseen. That's where diversity resides. Everyone is so different inside, so unique, so quick to get off at the next station. Is that what a city means? Is that what Tokyo trains mean? It's a writer's *koan* to ponder, process, and store for future narrative use. The train is a bookstore filled with stories being lived.

Some days, it seems all people do is peck peck peck on their little screens, lost in the bounce of colorful moving objects, but in fact, people often read. Their hands form little desks. Pecking means not reading, scrolling means skimming, but often, the eyes of the readers move calmly and regularly over the writing below. You can tell they're reading by how their eyes move, their neck angles, and their body unwinds. I like to see people engrossed by some inner drama or info intake. It's as amazing as watching someone dream.

I love being so close to the human form, the bodily manifestations of balance and proportion and beauty. I must turn away from it sometimes—it's too much anatomy. Pick a part of the human body you like best, and your ideal of it will appear within the week. The train becomes a life-drawing class, everyone posing, me sketching with mental pencils. How do you get people to look right? Well, they already do.

I marvel at Japanese consumer culture's power to keep everyone clothed so well. Tokyo's consumer kaleidoscope, with shapes and colors spinning into new patterns, is usually demure. Some days, it seems like it's all sensible, easy black. But then an outfit pops up that is color-filled and stunning. On the train, at least, bad taste is the frame around good taste.

Entering a Tokyo train is entering the consumer world of beer smiles, fake doctors, bright-colored hopes, and exclamatory faces. Our desires return to us in the overhead stretch of advertising. Video screens over the doors dish out snippets of news, weather, products, quizzes, anointing us all in the religion of buying that flows through every train car. "No thanks," I say to most of them.

There is more to the daily train journey than the consumer world and the to-and-from of work, play, or home. It is more than densely packed people. The train burrows into the heart of Japan, a hard-to-reach destination with its distancing psyche and odd habits. On the train, I am inside another level of Japanese society and culture. I'm surrounded by it. I'm as welcomed and rejected as anyone who pays their several hundred yen, but I have to figure it out for myself.

I find that in-it-but-not-of-it oddly comforting. I like that I'm not like everyone around me. It forces my foreignness back onto me. And yet we're on the same train, eyeing and pushing each other. It's comfortingly democratic—one person, one space. Train time is for comparing and contrasting, sorting through what matters and what doesn't. I close my eyes and feel the car burrow into the underground labyrinths of Japan, better than a Parisian café for people watching, better than channel surfing or internet scrolling for image overload.

I always try to see past the protective masks to get to the bullying boss, the pressure to pass exams, and the irritations of the day's impositions. For the duration of the ride, the worst worries of life are stilled and dormant, channeled into minute gestures. People primp their hair, fiddle with cellphones, check themselves in the reflection of the window, their concerns held like extra shopping bags. Watching people on Tokyo trains reminds me that it's not all Disney and light.

Some people on trains are blithely indifferent to train time and more resistant to observation and analysis. I study them too. Their masks are so complete, so effective. Not everyone's worried. Many accept their uniforms, their commute, the crowd, and their lives probably, without a care or thought, happy to do what needs to be done, to dress how one is supposed to dress as they travel across the city in the safe armor of conformity.

Or so it seems. Trains are all about seeming. I find it humbling to be just one more body, one more part of the crowd. And not much more. I like that self-effacing feeling of being repositioned in the urban universe of Tokyo. The train accepts all, none denied.

I feel jealous of the kids commuting to school, giggling over finger games, sharing video screens, plowing through thick adult legs, cramming test info, or napping in refusal. They move so easily on the train. I'm envious that it's such a natural environment for them. It's not quite that for me.

They know they belong on the train and always will. I belong differently—by choice.

Adults too, ease into the space. Friends, lovers, family, the entire spectrum of social dyads, drop into natural train mode. In the daytime, they're restrained. But at night, loud and loose with drink after a long *izakaya* chat, they talk, joke, touch each other's forearms, and release their thoughts in the last few minutes before their stop. I like that too. I try to overhear their whispered conversations. The tone of their voices harmonizes with the sounds of the train to make Tokyo train music, the calm echoes of the rigors of the Tokyo day.

Even when relaxing, though, the train is intense. Tokyo trains are the place where, as Thirdspace theorist Edward Soja said, "everything comes together... subjectivity and objectivity, the abstract and the concrete, the real and the imagined, the knowable and the unimaginable, mind and body, consciousness and the unconscious, everyday life and unending history." On Tokyo trains, the polarities resolve for the duration of the ride before disembarking to become tensions once again.

For me, the downtime on the train is a bit like the Jewish Sabbath, not a day but an hour or two of non-action. It's time to rethink, reflect, reimagine. I don't do anything. There's no cleaning, cooking, working, or turning on light switches. The train is a time to STOP *doing* things and start *being* something.

Maybe the urban planners had that in mind. I don't mean the government bureaucrats or cityscape architects, but the social forces that gave rise to the urban transit system. There's a demand from some deep well inside us for a space in motion, a place to be together where opposites meet, for the hope to get somewhere in life and return home again.

Without trains, Tokyo would not be itself, Tokyoites would not be themselves, and I wouldn't be myself in Tokyo. Bodies need moving, and minds need moving too. Among the millions of Tokyo spaces, the train is the one space I can't live without. I like taking the time to check in on humanity. I walk off the train restored, content that everyone's all right.

Can You See Fuji from There?

From my backyard, officially, I can see Mount Fuji. The iconic volcano rising from the plains southwest of Tokyo and Yokohama, is a stunning site no matter where you stand. But when I say I can see it from my house, I draw jealous gasps of "Really?" from Tokyoites. Saying you can see Mount Fuji from your house is like saying you have a view of Central Park to New Yorkers or a view of the harbor to Hong Kong-ers.

Everyone knows where Fuji is. After all, it's the most iconic image of Japan, coming in ahead of kimonos, chopsticks, and sushi. Because of the low plains surrounding it, Mount Fuji is visible from very far distances, and even as a small bump on the horizon it is instantly recognizable.

Everyone in the Tokyo area has a feeling for just where Mount Fuji is, like Muslims always know in which direction Mecca lies. Many people can catch the occasional glimpse of Fuji from where they pass by a break in apartment complexes, a window in an office walkway, or a small hill or elevated bridge.

But those are just quick peeks. It's not always easy to find a place in Tokyo or Yokohama where you can sit down to leisurely contemplate the setting sun throwing Fuji's elegant curves into evening relief. If it were an everyday thing, maybe there would be more contemporary poems and paintings of Fuji.

It would be hard to think of a new, fresh way to represent the iconic volcano. As it is, images of Fuji are relegated to color illustrations, ersatz woodblock print images, or fixed-up high-res photos. And to pop culture and advertising and names of companies and products. You can't really see Fuji because you see it all the time.

To be honest, to see Fuji from my house, I have to lean over the edge of the balcony or hoist myself up on my rickety cinderblock garden wall. It's a stretch, but it's there. Recently, a repair project on the power lines meant cutting down a bunch of trees. The lines went back up, but the trees stayed down. So now, I don't have to lean quite so far to catch a glimpse.

That view, even leaning and stretching for it, always packs a "wow." Set alone across the plains of Kanto, Mount Fuji is a unique bit of geography that rises up majestically, like a question to ponder. But is that because it's impressive in itself, or because I see some copy of Fuji's volcano lines somewhere during the day, on a tea bottle or truck siding? In that sense, you can see an image of Fuji almost everywhere anytime.

I can see more directly from around the corner, where a sliver of a hillside park offers a bench with a little note about this being yet another "Fujimi" spot. "Fujimi," or "place to see Mount Fuji," is a word describing all manner of places all through the Tokyo, Yokohama and Kanto region. There must be thousands, even millions, of Fujimi Roads, Fujimi Parks, Fujimi Hills, Fujimi Resorts, Fujimi Apartments. You get the idea. You could draw concentric lines of possible sighting spots.

That little moniker boosts not just the prestige, but also the price of whatever it attaches to. Many of those places still have an actual view of Mount Fuji that has not been blocked by building developments. Maybe you can see it from one side of the building, which justifies the name. Or more likely, you used to be able to see it fifty years ago, but not after the last apartment went up.

And yet, Tokyo and Yokohama sprang up from nothing after the war and plastered the skyline with whatever was immediately needed, not what was aesthetically optimal. Daily Fuji-viewing became shuttered by progress and one of the staple ironic tourist photos has long been a shot of factory smokestacks dotting the landscape from the Shinkansen tracks all the way to Fuji.

My very first view of Mount Fuji on the way to Kyoto shocked me. Even more factories dotted the plains, puffing out smoke, not inspiring many woodblock prints. You don't have to be a nihilist poet to figure out the symbolism there. In many ways, the irony of that first impression has remained.

My view out back is also congested. I have to edit out quite a bit of the view, not to mention all the obstructions in my head, to enjoy the elegance of the sun setting behind the poetry-inspiring slopes. To really see Fuji, I have to mentally erase the neighbor's house, a tangle of electric power lines, an ironwork scaffold for the lines, baseball field lights, and a couple of high-rise apartment buildings. After that, it's a clear view.

By this point in Japan's development, there are hardly any straight shots of Fuji left. Advertising photos and documentary footage have to be doctored to remove the clutter. Of course, you can travel to one of the gorgeous mountain lakes that surround Fuji like a necklace. But that means going on a special trip. It's worth it, of course, and people travel for just that reason. They buy expensive resort homes with picture windows. Fair enough.

Lots of people trek up and over it too, though the saying goes that everyone should climb Mount Fuji once, but only a fool would do it twice. Meanwhile, seeing images of Mount Fujii is something that happens incalculable times. It happens every day, though it's more often ignored as part of the background of life here, nothing special while the actual Fuji is something very special.

So, what is Mount Fuji? An image, a memory, a constructed symbol, an icon of value, power and constancy? Fuji has become an image in people's minds, one that can be seen only indirectly, or in pieces, never whole. Mount Fuji seems to rise as much from past images as from the plains below.

Maybe it was always so. The first mention of Fuji goes back to the *Manyoshu*, the oldest collection of poems in Japanese from the eighth century AD. Nowadays, the poems have been turned to advertising. I picture the samurai of old Edo riding out to the Musashino plains, where I live, for hunting, and stopping their horses to look at Fuji as it must once have been—untrammeled and unobstructed. But even the samurai are swept up into advertising, their own symbol of whatever the ad campaign might need.

Sitting to the west of Tokyo, Mount Fuji always seems like it is keeping its distance from the city. As if Tokyo came first, and the volcano afterward, in some inversion of land and culture, historical and geographical epochs. Or maybe Tokyo, knowing it can't compete, keeps its distance from Fuji, letting it remain where it was while the city sprang up in its own place for its own reasons.

Whatever it might mean, however it might be used and reused, I'll settle for my view of Mount Fuji out back. I gaze out at the slope, mistaking it for clouds on hazy or rainy days, and feel that it always comments, like a quiet relative, on the mega-city of Tokyo, reminding me that as amazingly huge and intriguingly developed as Tokyo is, there is always something else competing for our wonder.

Two Boys on the Train

Two boys bumped me as I was reading on the train last week. They were about nine or ten, with no school or shopping bag, in sports clothes, on the way home, I guessed, from soccer practice at their school sports ground a few stations away. Their giggling and push-pulling each other was punctuated by glances at one of the advertisements that blanket Tokyo trains.

I was tired and not in a people-watching mood, but I watched them anyway, without turning to see the ad, musing on how different their path home was from mine as a boy. My route home from school ran along a creek, which we called "the creek," and then meandered along lazy sidewalks, over a small footbridge, and past sycamore trees and wide lawns.

I started to watch as they whispered to each other, looking up and back. Tokyo trains are swathed in advertisements printed on paper about the size of a big computer screen. Beer, books, hotlines, tax info, shampoo, snacks, and everything that can be sold is slapped on paper and slipped on racks encircling the visual space of every train. If you glance around, there is no escape.

On my way home, we loved to take the sycamore tree seed balls, smash them open, and jam them down the shirt of an unsuspecting classmate. They itched like hell. Or at least we thought they did. And then we wrestled, fought, or played the same "grab-ass" these two Tokyo boys were playing on the train. Snowball fights across the iced-over creek were, for me, the highlight of winter. On Tokyo trains, there's room to stand, but you can't cock your arm to throw anything.

At one point, when we were about eleven or twelve, we started having battles with the girls. They always won since they were bigger than us at that point. Somehow, they would manage to get home, fill up water balloons, snatch bananas to smear in our hair, and run back to where the roads diverged before we got there. We sometimes had to go the long way a couple of blocks over to avoid them. Of course, we didn't really want to avoid them. We wanted something else which we couldn't define.

That could all happen because we walked home in a glorious child-only world, far from the eyes of adults. Cars drove by, but no one we knew. Or rarely. We were free for the twenty dawdling minutes it took us to walk home, or even an hour if we got into things, fights, talks, or games. We loved the rain, so we could splash in puddles and throw worms at each other. We had space, time, snow, sycamore balls, bugs, and other kids. What more could you want?

The two Tokyo boys seemed to me trapped on the train home. They kept scuffling and drawing glances from the adults, tired from work and in no mood for their fooling around if it meant being bumped into. Even when they got off the train, there would be people all along their route home. They were monitored. How much trouble could they get into? Their mistakes didn't look like they'd be big ones.

I turned to look at the ad the boys kept glancing at and whispering about. It was for Playboy magazine. The ad was the usual: full-breasted women in bikinis, a sidebar of other women's cleavages, their faces smiling or pouting or faking innocence. All around them was text in splashy fonts trumpeting the writing. It was not much in this day and age of internet porn, but the boys could not get their eyes off the ad.

They were looking and whispering, whispering and looking. I strained to hear what they said, but they spoke too softly. But I knew what they were saying. I had said the same things myself. It was on my grade school walk home that some classmate revealed the Playboy photo he'd torn out of his father's magazine. It was a wonder to us at the time, even folded in quarters and wrinkled at the edges. We huddled on the rocks on the bank of the creek and looked at the images of women the Playboy editors had concocted for us. It was a rare and momentous event that I remember all these years later.

Were these boys' reactions the same as mine—awe at my first nude? Did these two Tokyo boys feel the same stirrings, sneaking glances up at an advertisement they were still too short even to reach? Surrounded by tired commuters watching them knowingly, appalled or indifferent, was that boyhood glance as naïve, curious, and desiring for those boys as it had been for me?

Though we were separated by decades, cultures, languages, and surroundings, it startled me to re-confront the boyish interest in sex and women's bodies. So far away from where I had seen that first nude was the exact same magazine, spinning out the exact same headlines, same attitudes, and same poses. Even the word splashed across the cover—"nude"—is used in Japanese (pronounced "new-dough"). Was that what coming home with friends meant—the discovery of the world, inner and outer?

My sycamores and creek in Kansas could not be more different from a Tokyo train car and platform. The 1960s and the 2020s, a sleepy suburb and a thriving city, open spaces and cramped trains all seem a gap too huge to bridge. Yes, we both played soccer, came home with friends, wrestled, joked, and felt confused, but those boys' and my youth's culture, language, education, and upbringing bore little similarity.

And yet, in the middle of both was a deceptively tantalizing, but still awe-inspiring representation of the female body. It had fallen on them, as with me, before being conscious of it, and the need to look rose, no doubt, from inside us with the same yearnings and confusions. Were we both ensnared in the same mess or were we both just kids waking up to inner impulses?

Both cultures are unduly strict about certain issues, but impossibly lax about others. Those boys and I were similarly brought into a society with a potent media that sought to shape our views and push us in directions we might not otherwise choose. Maybe the media, not our boyish desire, is the universal? Even in my old creek, before the deluge of media satiated our lives, the media could find its way into our consciousness. In Tokyo, it's impossible to avoid.

When they ran out the door at their station, I was left wondering why our cultures, so thorough at mediating and shaping our experiences, couldn't have given us the first view of something so magnificent in any better way. But no one else on the train even seemed to notice, and I turned back to reading and listening to music, left to ponder another train moment that made me feel connected to humanity and slightly repulsed and removed from it at the same time. It was a normal commute.

More than Sending a Letter

Every time I go to the Japanese post office, I'm overwhelmed. Stepping inside a Japanese post office presents an array of options that are hard to fully identify, much less fully take advantage of. You can run your entire household, perhaps your entire life, from inside any post office. Japanese post offices are made for multitasking. Whenever I go inside, I end up with sensory overload.

It's not just stamps and packages. Japan's post offices are all banks too. My American compartmentalizing mind thinks of those as separate, but in Japan, they go together as easily as raw fish and rice. I've often taken a number from the postal section and another from the banking section and sat down to wait my turn at both.

The Japanese postal bank was once said to have the largest savings deposits in the world. I'm not sure if that's true, but it seems like it. You can quickly set up savings accounts for various purposes, though no American-style checking account system exists. They also have retirement and pension accounts, college savings, and pretty much anything else any bank would offer. You can send money, pay bills, pay rent, buy insurance, or file a tax return. The walls, counters, and trays are filled with signs for all manner of activities, each one of them doable with just a word to the clerks. It's a transition point of goods, money, and forms, all of it handled with brisk efficiency.

I like how the services are aimed at us small people, not big investors. The services are mostly for grandparents trying to encourage their grandchildren to learn how to save. You can get a piggy bank for kids or set up a college fund. It's at the very heart of Japan's frugality, a way to appreciate even the small coin that might have gone astray. That said, the interest rates on accounts are so low that it's hard to see the wisdom in letting inflation surge while your postal savings languish. But maybe it's not the reality that counts, but the idea.

The post office is also an information center. There are posters and leaflets about everything from money and finances to reminders about sending gifts at gift-giving season, new stamp issues, free breast cancer checks, changes in prices and policies, and, well, there isn't time to read all of them because you're shuffled along to the counter fairly efficiently. Pamphlets are neatly lined up on counters, ready to be taken home for further perusal. The staff know the information and can direct you to it faster than a digital assistant on your computer.

Whenever I go inside, it feels like a community center. It's always humming, everyone aware of everyone else but not really interacting with them. Many people come in only for the ATMs in the outer section. Bikes are parked outside, retirees wait on benches, mothers bounce their babies, and office people bring mass mailings in neat folders. Like the train, the post office is a great common space. Everyone uses it, and everyone feels like it's set up for them, which it is. Whether you're setting up a tax-free pension, buying age-specific insurance, stamps, or envelopes (a hundred types of envelopes), there is something for everyone.

When I first came to Japan, it was the one place where I understood all the rules, which can otherwise be incomprehensibly complex. There is no doubt or hesitation in the post office. Everything is answered concretely, directly, and efficiently.

The post office is also a place to sit down. The functional sofas and soft chairs are well-used, but clean and neat. If a few older people sit longer than they strictly need to, no one seems too bothered. Offices are conveniently located near train stations and, in my case, near my home, but it is always where a steady stream of people already go. Or maybe they go along those streets because the post office is there. The place feels like it's from another era but still hanging on, like a road made for foot traffic in the Edo era. It just persists.

I'm always amused by the gifts since I never really entered into the card-sending and gift-giving relations that keep Japan stitched together. You can easily send New Year's cards and *Ochugen* (summer) and *Oseibo* (winter) presents, crabs from Hokkaido, ham from Yokohama, towels, soap, and housewarming presents. They are good quality, perhaps not as fancy as you'd get in a department store, but that's not the point. The point is sending something to keep a social connection or to help someone out. The post office makes such social tasks much less of a burden.

The clerks, traditionally all women, but now with more men, are efficient and informed. They wear neat uniforms, not as formal as banks, and have name tags, though it's hard to read them as they are in constant motion. Whatever you ask for, it seems to click some inner route, and they head right for it. They immediately hand over the special forms for sending overseas and give me a terse explanation of what to fill in. I go to one of the counters, pull a pen from the nice holder, and get to work. I don't want to waste their time. Their efficiency is infectious.

Occasionally, if I ask for something special, they have to go back to the supervisors who sit at desks at the back, ready to answer anything. I love it when they have to check as they open huge cabinets with rows of thick binders at the back. They plunk them down on their desk and flip through the pages for how to file a form with the US tax office (yes, required, unbelievably for all US citizens) or how to send a package to India. I want to laugh as the information is always there and always in detail. Often, they will hand me a printout with more information than I need. I always politely take the printout and mutter my thanks. It's so organized, it's Marie Kondo before Marie Kondo.

It's like a general store from the nineteenth century, a sort of internet before the internet. But it also seems to resist the recent move to do everything online. There's a materiality to everything there. Every time I ask a question, they hand me a paper copy explaining the answer and then some. Sure, you can do things online, prepare a mailing address, or register a package, but there's a pleasure in touching things the post office promotes that feels comforting. And I'm sure it is even more comforting for older people who are used to doing everything by hand. Pamphlets, flyers, information, colorful little stamps, everything is *in hand*. It all seems to resist moving online. It revels in paper. I like that.

It often takes longer than I like, so I have to adjust to a slow-life attitude. I use two different post offices, a larger one close to the train station and a local one a short bike ride from my house. At the closer one, I have to schedule extra time. They remember me. I'm a special project of theirs, it seems. I can't just go in and send a letter. I have to discuss the options. They always encourage me to send it the cheapest way, but I'm usually in a hurry and opt for the quickest, even if it costs more. I have to argue with them to spend my money. They push me toward the cheapest option, eyeing me like some profligate spender who doesn't know better. Which, I guess, I am.

During the pandemic, the explanations got more complicated. Overseas shipping slowed down and even stopped at a couple of points. The post office clerks apologized to me profusely, as if it were their fault a package couldn't get where it was going for several unpredictable weeks. They kept handing me the most recent flyer with new arrival estimates. I had to deflect their apology and say it wasn't Japan's fault that shipping was slowed down everywhere. But they seemed to feel it was their part in connecting Japan to the larger world. They took responsibility for the delay.

Maybe they had taken me under their wing because I had talked to one of the clerks about her daughter. As I am a university professor, every parent I meet wants to ask about entrance exams, study plans, and the mindset of young people, which is always a mystery to parents. This one clerk had asked me questions over the course of years. I would get ensnared in dispensing advice and listening to her concerns as the other clerks listened in.

And also, I suspect, at the smaller post office, they're always a little bored. I'm often the youngest one in there. For some older people, I guess it's their big outing for the day, a calm, soothing place for them. Even though the post office is a world of clear, precise rules, it's also like a community from another age, a kinder, closer one that cares about doing things right, not for the sake of the rule, but for the people who are helped. It soothes me to be in a place built on such certainty, clarity, and calm. Then, when I'm done, it's back out to Tokyo.

Tokyo Open and Closed

As a foreigner, living in Tokyo is easier than ever before. It's not just that I can now find cheese and wine easily. Even more amazingly, Japanese people like cheese just as much as I do. Western coffee shops have proliferated near every train station, and foreign streaming channels have taken over every screen. Even at traditional hanami parties, people consume as much foreign wine as Japanese sake to celebrate the spring cherry blossoms!

Tokyo has become more Westernized, but that's not what I think is the best change over the last couple of decades. Westernization has a good and bad side. Lots of odd customs and habits filter into Japan, island nation though it is. So, when I say it's easier for me to live in Tokyo now than twenty years ago, I mean Tokyo has become more open.

Tokyo now offers everyone, cheese-lovers or not, more choices about how to live, work, and relax than in the past. The range of lifestyle choices and ways of thinking has expanded so that people can live more freely. My students are no longer locked into an escalator system that shuffles them along a chute from high school to entrance exam to university to work. The variety of experiences, artistic, cultural, and just living, has expanded tremendously in recent years despite a slowing down during the pandemic. Tokyo is not just a place; it's also an idea that keeps unfolding into greater choice, mental space, and receptivity.

Of course, there are still plenty of rules. Japanese culture can feel stifling, and more young Japanese leave to make their lives in other countries. In my seminar alone, one or two students head abroad every year to seek fame and fortune or a better work-life balance. More than other world cities, Tokyo has maintained traditional social rules and customs. Women have made progress, but not nearly enough. In many ways, Tokyo has changed more slowly than other big cities, saddled by a vast reserve of traditional ideas and unquestioned practices. But it's also changing steadily.

For foreigners, surviving in Tokyo requires learning the onslaught of Japanese rules and practices. The more complex the interaction, the more complicated the rules become. In Tokyo, social rules determine how to shop in a store, order in a restaurant, stand on a train, or just ask for directions. For foreigners, the tremendous number of expectations can be exasperating and demanding.

You can break those rules, and Tokyoites will not say much directly, but they signal their displeasure with sighs, stares, frowns, and an entire vocabulary of displeased body language. And no matter how often you break a rule, the rules remain. That closed side of Tokyo can be wearying.

To me, though, the constraints of Japanese culture always seem to be in a standoff with the openness of Tokyo's progressive trends. If Tokyo is as much an idea as a location, it is an idea often divided against itself. The open side of Tokyo stares down the conformist side like two sumo wrestlers in a long *shikiri*, poised for the initial charge at each other.

In past years, if I stepped into a small, out-of-the-way *izakaya*, the staff often greeted me with wide-eyed panic and a worried look away from the customers. Would I speak Japanese? Would I like Japanese food? Could I follow the *izakaya* rules? Would I demand wine and cheese? Changing the flow of the restaurant's standard practices to accommodate a foreign customer was often met with reluctance.

Nowadays, though, stores and restaurants are vastly more receptive and less concerned about an unusual person stepping into their midst. If anything, I miss being noticed all the time. I feel ignored. Nowadays, people worry not about my foreignness disrupting the smooth Japanese flow, but whether I will appreciate the beauty of their place. They want to explain how special the appetizer is or how high-tech some new eyeglasses are. I am no longer disrupting the harmony. Tokyo's harmony now encompasses diversity.

Even more surprising these days, people will speak to me in English or offer an English menu in many places. Accommodation has been planned for. The arrival of a foreigner is now expected. Wait staff and store clerks never seem to mind if I ask a few extra questions that no Japanese would need to ask. That receptivity is not entirely new, but it's much more widespread. In the past, there were pockets of acceptance. For me, that meant jazz clubs, my students, select friends, and bars and restaurants where I went repeatedly. But now, it's almost everywhere.

Conversations with strangers in Tokyo used to be rather dull—predictable, I mean. I was constantly asked whether I could adapt to Tokyo life. It used to be a big mystery to most people why I would choose to live in Tokyo since I had not been born here, transferred here, or married here. That I could not adapt to living here was the default assumption. My questioners could not understand how any non-

Tokyoite would end up living in Tokyo.

Now, though, Tokyoites understand the appeal of Tokyo as a place to live, work, love, and play—and not just for those assigned here by birth, work, or relationship. The pleasure and wonder of living in Tokyo seem evident to most Tokyoites now. That's partially because millions of visitors a year are flowing through the city, but also because of a new awareness of Tokyo. It's now a world city, not just an urban growth in an archipelago far from the action. The action is here now.

Magazines have selected Tokyo as one of the planet's most livable cities. Michelin stars have been dished out to restaurants. TV shows interview foreigners about why they came to Japan. That adds up and changes the mindset from "What are you doing here?" to "What do you like best here?" Tokyoites have a sense of pride born of a newly appreciative view of their city. The idea of Tokyo has expanded and loosened, and as that has happened, it has become a place not just to end up but, more importantly, to choose to be in.

All that is an opening of the Japanese mindset, a loosening from past strictures. Japanese culture is a conservative one. That hasn't changed. But large cities are also cosmopolitan, and of all the large cities in Asia, Tokyo is the most cosmopolitan. The world came to Tokyo during the bubble years in the 1990s, but that was more about Japan's economic position. Now, it's about Japan's cultural position.

The cycle of opening has spun in larger circumferences, opening to the world. More than any other factor, animation has become immensely popular abroad. That makes non-Japanese fascinated with Japan. And that, in turn, makes many, even most, Japanese people fascinated with why they would be fascinated. That might not be a tremendous liberal shift, but it's a start.

In a recent conversation with a taxi driver when we pulled near Shinagawa Station, I complained about the disorganized taxi line outside the station. "Ah, now you're thinking like a Tokyo-*jin*," the driver said. I took that as a compliment, one that would have been impossible in years past, when the driver would have said something defensive like, "Well, there's a lot of people and cars in Tokyo," as if I hadn't noticed. However, the fact that the driver and I both had the same complaint meant we were not on opposite sides of a closed cultural line, but the city mindset had opened enough to let my opinion in. That's a change from the past.

And yet still, I often sense the cold wind of strict rules or traditional obligations that limit how freely foreigners—and Japanese—live. But when I feel the iron grip of those constraints, I know that I can always shift my attention towards the open sides of Tokyo, to the music clubs, the small movie theaters, the odd fads, the unexpected conversations, and the many different ways of thinking, working, living and enjoying life in the city. In the past, it was either inside or outside, but the opening of that boundary means Tokyo's life choices are wider than ever.

And in that, there is openness. The sheer range of human choices pushes the city's life into greater openness. The freedom and openness of Asia's most unconstrained megalopolis—Tokyo—are often hidden but always waiting.

By this, I mean that I can always find really good cheese.

Photograph Everything

To know a Japanese female, whether as family, friend, teacher, colleague, or lover, is to be photographed repeatedly. Japanese women love to take photographs, though they are sometimes shy about it initially. However, once they get over their shyness, they take photos of everything. Cameras are like a pair of glasses or a magnifying glass that helps Japanese women see, understand, and remember exactly what happens in their lives. They stare at themselves with the camera, checking their bangs or teasing their hair. Then, when it's all re-set just right, they snap another selfie.

Every critical life experience, from school activities to Christmas dates to a lonely, delicious meal, is recorded in photos. Putting on a kimono is done more for the photo than for the coming-of-age ritual or graduation ceremony. When Japanese women pack their bags, the first thing they put in is their cell phone. When they upgrade their cell phones, it's usually to get a better camera function. It's a basic life necessity.

At a seminar outing, one of my students told the group, with tears in her eyes, how she broke her cell phone and lost one entire year's worth of photos! That was before the cloud when photos were kept on the phone, not in cloud storage. It was the worst experience of her life, she said. Everyone sympathized, trying to imagine the years of photos ripped away. The automatic save function was developed to avoid such disasters.

Japanese women's photos serve the same purpose as

business cards: they set up connections and confirm relationships. With my students, most of whom are women, I always take a teacher-student photo. It becomes proof that their teacher was a foreigner. We are locked in our educational dyad forever. The photo is more important than their grade or a comment on an essay. Our photo affirms our teacher-student relationship, made truer than by conversation, grades, or discussions. It's a mnemonic for the future.

With friends, it is the same. Boyfriends cannot be called a boyfriend until a complete photographic record exists. Japanese women demand to get photographed with people they are close to. It means something important to them. Another friend told me that until she broke up with her boyfriend, they took a photo together at the same "print club" photo machine every month on their monthly anniversary. It was retro-cool but also a sign of a deep connection. To look inside the photo memory of a Japanese woman's cellphone is to see all the intimate details of her life.

Men take photography seriously as a job or a hobby, but women chronicle Japanese life by integrating photo-taking into the natural flow of their lives. In the future, when historians want to understand this century's actual experience and social relations, they will turn to women's photos, not men's. Instead of sewing clothes or weaving baskets, Japanese women have made a new folk art (*mingei*) for our times—photos.

Don't Japanese men take photos? Of course, they do, but Japan might be one of the few countries where the gender divide is less an argument and more of a difference. My male students take tons of photos, often initiating the photo-taking at important outings. But the women linger after the first official photos and click off a few extra shots to be sure the evening's drinking party or the end of the semester doesn't go unrecorded. Photo addiction is more personal than gendered, of course, but the percentages lean toward the female side.

When women work as professional photographers, they have different working styles altogether. I love to watch women photographers at concerts or special events. They have patience for the right moment to shoot, knowing intuitively the exact second when a singer will smile, or the wedding cake will drop onto the groom's cheek. If all of that sounds like a stereotype, it seems to be the case just the same. Covering the jazz scene for years, I've seen many professional women photographers who take a serious, yet somehow very feminine, approach to their work.

But for the most part, women don't like hauling around all the big lenses and heavy accessories. Instead, they like light, easy-to-use cameras because they want to grab them any time and all the time! They never take photos from a distance, but always up close. "Wait a second," spoken with a camera waving in one's hand, is a command followed by the entire population of the country. People freeze and wait as the photographer moves closer at the just-right angle. Taking a photo is a way of touching. Touching is rarer in Japan than in Western and most Asian cultures. When touch is socially restrained, photos bring people into contact, both physically and photographed.

The photos of women carry deep, complex tensions. They are not aiming to capture the rich hues of a flower, the speed of a train, or the structure of a building; instead, they want photos of human situations with the people central.

They want pictures of inner emotions, even if those emotions are posed and temporary. Of course, women also take photos of special meals, a neighborhood cat, or lights strung up on trees, but those photos are always taken from their perspective, showing their relation to those special things. They are a way of reaching. They are a way of reading the world.

Photos express women's unique points of view, becoming an emotional outlet and a record of past feelings. They cannot be censored, are not subject to social strictures, and can be saved secretly in vast electronic storage chambers in cellphones, computers, and backup disks. They form a sort of inner freedom, far from the constraints of Japanese society. Photos remain hidden inside, safe and secure, folded like a kimono from one's grandmother. Knowing the images are there is a relief, like having money in the bank.

This constant photo-taking from Japanese women sometimes gets a bit tiring. Stopping to take a photo interrupts dinner, an outing, an event, or a walk down the street. At all those times, there's always a bit of acting in photos too. Women rarely take un-posed, natural photos, but like a movie director staging a scene, get everyone to stop what they are doing, hold up their beer mug, and gesture in a forced way. It seems like a mask, but it's a mask that expresses feeling. The genuine emotion can be seen inside the pose, behind the mask.

Every year at graduation, students dress in colorful *hakama* and do their hair for the hundreds of photos the day involves. The last day of class also demands photos, but the official graduation day is serious photo-taking. As the teacher, I enter hundreds of photos throughout graduation day in various combinations, with the entire class, with two best friends, with a single student, relaxed, formal, and every position in between. I pose and pose, and my image flies away into hundreds of storage facilities and photo-organizing apps. In that sense, I'm all over Tokyo.

Photos are a visual force that works to deepen relationships, to remember events, and to bring people, literally, together. Photos are an excuse to push together along the tatami-mat floor of a drinking place, to snuggle into place, to put one's shoulder against someone else's, to feel their warmth and smell their scent, even if only for a second. While open touching is rare in Japanese society, scrunching into the frame of a photo is how people become physically close. Taking a photo involves being together in a frame and, more importantly, existing together.

I think of photos in Japan as a kind of national smiling therapy. That is no small deal in a country with one of the highest suicide rates in the world. Japanese women know the importance of allowing everyone to express positive inner feelings when so much of Japanese life tends to grab feelings by their necks and jam them back deep inside. While some poses seem practiced and forced, a photo is *the* moment to express true feelings. It's rare to see a genuine smile during a typical Tokyo day. Commuters, shop clerks, office personnel, and students in large classes all wear impassive masks. But nearly every photo has a beaming, heartfelt smile. Photos work an alchemical magic. Women are in charge of the transformation.

The one singular moment in Japanese life, when everyone is the happiest, freest, and most beautiful, is that one moment when a Japanese woman picks up a camera and utters that magical command: "Smile!"

Next Door Close

Tearing down and re-building a house without disturbing what's next door requires a lot of planning in a city where you can reach out a window and touch the neighbors' outside wall. Tokyo is so packed that some buildings are first built from the top floor, which is cranked up with jacks so the next floor can be constructed below, and it, in turn, gets raised. There *are* open spaces between buildings throughout the city, but not many, and none wide.

I'm always amazed at how construction sites can work in such narrow confines. I stop and watch them from time to time. Cranes, mega-trucks, and long flatbeds can hardly make a turn in the streets. Tokyo is crowded humanly and architecturally, so when a building is torn down, and a new one is built, it requires another level of planning not to bother the buildings or people on either side. It's like getting dressed in a toilet stall.

I learned more about that than I cared to after my next-door neighbor rang my doorbell one day with a young man in tow. They handed me towels, a traditional gift when moving into homes, and told me they would move out, tear down their house, and build a new one. It all sounded OK chatting by the front gate. But I was to become "the house next door."

A few weeks later, they got started. I stood out and watched the house being torn down. I snapped a few photos as the old wood house went down with no more than the scream of scrunched wood. The rip-tear of piping, flooring, and roofing carried over to our house for days. A Tokyo construction site had come to us.

The smell started soon after the first day. The house had decades of dust, mold, and toxic substances that started floating through the air. It was a fifty-some-year-old home, well-kept, but it was made for another time. My wife wore a face mask all day, but we sneezed for two weeks straight. They hosed down the place, cleaning up in front. The next day, the jackhammering started.

It's impossible to have jackhammering next door without hunching your shoulders and looking for an exit. We started finding excuses to run errands to get away. But it was during the pandemic, and I taught from home. The noise filtered into my online classes. The trucks began rumbling into our street around seven, and work started at eight, but the jackhammer operators seemed to take an hour to get started around nine. Perhaps it took an hour to set their ear protection devices properly. Every jackhammered chunk of concrete rattled the earth—and my teeth.

We live on a dead-end where the houses are raised about chest-high from street level. I'd always liked those few stairs up. However, the stone walls and pavement also serve as an echo chamber for every sound. On normal days, all that gets amplified is dogs barking, elderly walkers shouting, kids going to the park, or the garbage truck. The jackhammering, though, rattled down the concrete corridor with ear-shattering power. Aurally, the next-door home was very close.

Once that was done, there was a tranquil ground dedication ceremony in Shinto style. The priest consecrated the ground, chanted sutras, and spiritually prepped the earth for building. It was the only respite for months.

After the ceremony sank in, foundation work began. As the next contingent of workers arrived to dig up the dirt for the concrete foundation, the rich smells of soil buried for decades wafted over to our house. It was better than the mold and dust, but overpowering in its way—first, the ears; second, the nose. The earth-moving backhoe bucked like a wild horse, shaking our house like an earthquake.

Once the earth was ready, the concrete trucks arrived. They were very polite about taking up most of the street. It only took a few minutes for the concrete mixer to back up enough when we needed to squeeze our bikes out. Another brief lull let the concrete dry.

The construction company supervisors stopped by again with a map of the four houses at our end of the street. They politely explained they would bring a crane to hoist materials up and into place. They apologized for the inconvenience and drew a little diagram of where the goods would be transported over the corner of our house.

I've seen cranes all over Tokyo, most of them multiple stories tall, so I couldn't imagine one on my little street where two cars can barely pass. I imagined the crane swinging a bundle of pipes, a stack of wood, or maybe a box of tools.

Then, on Christmas day, it started. I told the construction company rep that they had to stop work by the afternoon at around three as I was having a Christmas party. They agreed and said they'd finish before the party started. And they did, actually, on time. The workers even wished us "Merry Christmas" as they headed home early.

But before that, my Christmas present was the sight of prefabricated 2.5-ton ferroconcrete walls swinging over the house. The trucks arrived early, the one-story-tall walls strapped and leaning for balance on a large rack set in the bed of a truck. The crane, already in place, dropped straps to fasten around the walls. It was all set. The crane hoisted the first concrete wall, swung it over the trees in my front garden, and then over the corner of my house.

Until then, I wasn't quite sure what the crane involved, but yes, the walls veered at an angle over our house before setting down into the concrete foundation. As I grilled turkey in the backyard, I thought it was the strangest Christmas I'd ever had. The good news was there were only thirty walls.

Despite my fascination with construction and a well-developed trust in Japanese safety regulations, it was impossible to watch concrete walls swinging over the house without imagining them dropping and demolishing the bedroom, bathroom, and kitchen. If they fell toward our house, they'd also take out the bath, living room, and toilet.

It takes time to move and position concrete walls, so for the week-plus we had concrete flying overhead, my wife and I took quick showers and stayed on the other side of our house. We'd dash into the kitchen for food and then retreat to relative safety on the other side of the house. I'd always taken a boyish delight in watching construction sites around Tokyo. But I never realized how far they were from the sidewalk or station platform until the construction site was close enough to touch out the window.

Even though the crane operator and the guys guiding the walls into place were professionals, their skill in jiggling concrete walls into the concrete mold below was little comfort. They used crowbars to set the wall in place, deftly propped struts into preset holes, and used a trowel to smooth the wet concrete that spilled out between the base and the wall. It was marvelously choreographed. The workers had obviously done this a million times on a million walls. But why did that not comfort me?

One day, when they took a lunch break, I chatted with them as they ate instant noodles and onigiri rice balls and sipped hot tea on the half-done first floor. They had been working all morning right below two tons of concrete that they pushed into place by hand and crowbar. But at lunch, they seemed as carefree as any other workers, laughing, smoking, and chatting.

Perhaps they had never watched American cartoons, where the characters are routinely squashed by anvils, houses, wrecking balls, *and* falling walls. After being squashed, the flat, 2-D characters pop up, dance awkwardly for a second, and spring back to three dimensions. Eventually, the walls were all in place. All I could think was about their earthquake-proofing.

Finally, there were some quiet days when the workers did whatever they wanted inside the house. At times, I couldn't see or hear much, just whispers of assembly. But then there was a week of drilling and smoothing concrete, which comes in a couple of decibels below jackhammer level. A prefabricated house seemed to need an extraordinary amount of drilling and smoothing.

We didn't need to set our alarms for months. The trucks backed into place every morning right on time, just before eight. The trucks' automatic backup warning signal, which beeped and broadcast "*Backu shimasu*" in Japanese, became our call to rise and shine. In that sense, we were part of the project—as witnesses.

At long last, two months later than the initial schedule

promised, the scaffolding clanked down and was loaded onto the trucks. Taking apart scaffolding involves a lot of shouting as the poles are passed down. "Last chance to destroy our home," I wanted to shout. But their scaffold disassembly skill kept the poles from smashing into our windows an arms-length away. Our place had survived with only one loosened roof tile and a lot of anxiety.

And a week or two later, the neighbors moved back in. They've been quiet ever since. And I've felt closer to them than ever.

Advice in Tokyo

The biggest relief for me at the end of every Tokyo summer is not the first cool breeze of the fall, but the end of summer advice. Perhaps because I am redder-faced and sweatier than everyone else, I'm a magnet for advice about heat and humidity. Everyone I talk to in Tokyo keeps telling me how to cool down: drink ice water, drink hot tea, eat *maccha* ice, don't eat anything iced, eat cooked eel, sit by the fan, or don't sit by the fan.

Well-intentioned as all this advice is, it gets tiring to take it all in. I want to follow all the advice I heard this summer about getting rid of mold, putting up awnings, and staying hydrated, but following advice entails work. One of the ways Tokyoites make life smoother and easier is through a constant exchange of advice. It's a conversational template.

The advice I used to get when I first came to Tokyo was more about where to go and where to eat, but the internet has taken that over. Back then, advice was necessary to find restaurants, bars, interesting walks, and hidden historical treasures. One of the best pieces of advice I received when I first came to Tokyo was: never eat in a place with no menu out front (you can't afford it), and never eat in a place with dust on the food display (it won't be good). I've religiously followed those two pieces of advice and have never had a bad meal.

Advice involves more than pointing out the likelihood of rain, so take an umbrella. It encompasses daily details—the best place to do your banking, where to shop for anything, the best way to clean whatever, how to use stored points, and always how to get a lower price on everything from tickets to bicycles to homes. Some advice comes off as scolding for not knowing better, but almost all focus on doing things the right way. Without advice, you might do things the wrong way, which is one of Japan's most grievous social mistakes. Advice keeps you on the right track.

Even in Tokyo's fast-paced, anonymous life, advice continues to be exchanged on a small, human scale. There's advice for almost any situation. One day, I couldn't believe I was listening to a friend tell me where to get cheaper bags of ice. Advice is similar to the many *kotowaza* proverbs of Japanese culture. As those proverbs become less common, the advice seems to take its place to guide humanity through Tokyo life.

Some of this advice is helpful and true, but because there's so much all the time, I feel skeptical about it and a bit weary. My neighbor's advice about growing tomatoes is always right. All mine have withered, and hers are going strong. I appreciate that. But when Japanese friends point at the weeds in my backyard and tell me they make medicinal tea, I start squirming. I give *them* advice—take some weeds home with you if it's so healthy. They never do.

Other Tokyo advice seems to steer me too far away from what feels best. Is standing right under the air conditioning fan on the train that bad for me, as one office staffer at my school insisted? I sway back and forth, following the fan's direction to get my head as cool as possible! I feel better. What's wrong with that? But they were just repeating something they heard or read in the newspaper. Japanese newspapers, by the way, are filled with advice.

I guess there is a better way to wash rice, though I've already forgotten one of my friend's wife's detailed directions. Push the rice into the water with the palms of both hands, rinse...well I've already forgotten it, but I haven't forgotten the experience of receiving advice. There's always a judgment tucked inside, but how am I supposed to know how to wash rice? Should I be ashamed of my rice-washing ignorance?

The constant patter of advice in Tokyo makes me feel like my grandmother is following me around, fussing: "Here's how you get the fish smell out of the kitchen...Here's how you...." Or maybe everyone carries their grandmothers around in their heads. Each additional piece of advice only makes me want to find more advice to calm my worries about the last bit of advice.

Oscar Wilde said, "The only thing to do with good advice is to pass it on. It is never of any use to oneself." Tokyoites seem to live that piece of advice perfectly, passing on advice to others like unwanted *ochugen* summer gift-giving gifts. There is only so much you can soak up, much less follow—the rest you must delete from your brain by telling someone else.

I can't imagine where it all comes from, but I guess it's from mothers educating their children. "Here's the best way, here's my advice, listen to me" must be constant refrains in Japanese homes. Mothers feel it's their duty to give the right advice to their children, and that spreads through society. Teachers dispense advice as their primary pedagogical purpose.

In America, the default setting is much more about figuring things out on your own. My students often want step-by-step guides to reading more deeply, writing papers, giving presentations, or improving their English. However, the American point of view is much more about finding your own set of personal practices. Americans, like Oscar Wilde, resist advice. "I can do it myself!" is an American way of thinking. But Japanese are always open to advice and, in fact, welcome it. And maybe feel lost without it.

Advice feels like folk wisdom: fairly sensible, slightly surprising, and meant in a kindly way. It's always a little out-of-date, always a bit over-detailed. It's a way of controlling the small things in life. When people give me advice, I feel like I'm no longer lost in a gigantic, postmodern megalopolis, but temporarily transported to a small village where everyone exchanges homey tips and earthy suggestions as they gather water at the village well.

Eventually, there will be a cellphone app for every part of Tokyo life that needs assistance. There probably always is. I suppose I could get by in Tokyo without advice, and I'll confess I always half-listen. I like that advice is about sharing, connecting, focusing on minute activities, and trying to solve little problems.

Life in Tokyo has many comforts but many irritations too. Advice tries to steer you from the latter to the former. So, I reluctantly accept a friendly tip now and again since it feels like a form of affection and a time-saver, both of which are in short supply. Tokyo life needs counsel, encouragement, and the occasional warning. It's hard to get by without it.

Part Two
Seasons and Rituals

Introduction

Rituals are an important part of Japanese life in general and life in Tokyo in particular, but making sense of them is not always easy. Joseph Campbell argued that rituals are a representation of a myth, and myths lead us to a deeper wisdom. I hope that might be true, but rituals can also lead us away from depth and strand us on the surface of life. The rituals of life in Tokyo are always easy to avoid. The city hums along at all hours, indifferent to holidays, activities, important days, and the long history of ritual. The season is always noticed, but often ignored.

Some rituals, though, maintain their presence and draw people in time and time again. Me included! I've never felt the rituals of Japanese culture too imposing. That's because I am in but not *of* Japan. I'm pushed along by the seasons, but not stuck inside the seasonal rituals. I can skip sending gifts or New Year's cards, and no one will think anything too bad of me. I can bow at the wrong time or apologize at the totally wrong time, and the Japanese write it off as me being a foreigner not knowing the correct ritual. I'm excused.

Other bigger rituals strike me as less a ladder down into wisdom as steps towards a higher beauty. That's the feeling I have with the writings in this section, "Rituals." Even that word has become infused with a hint of criticism, which is too bad because it misses the pleasure in repetition and the joy in knowing what to do and how to do it. Rituals are carried out with pleasure and meaning as often as not.

Many non-Japanese who make their home in Japan incorporate Japanese rituals into their lives in profound ways. I'm not one of those types. I enjoy looking at the rituals around me and taking them on board as fascinating experiences that can transform my thoughts and feelings and make my life richer and fuller. If that sounds a bit selfish, I suppose it is. But so be it. I want to give back through the writing.

Tokyo's rituals are resilient and unimposing, making participation easy without becoming ritualized. I like that flexibility. It fits the words better. It fits me better. I can participate, observe up close, watch from far away, or position myself where I want.

Missing Meishi

By the end of the pandemic, the diameters of my social circles hadn't budged. I met no one new. I know that because I didn't acquire any new *meishi* name cards. I didn't give or receive the small cards, about the size of three fingers and loaded with contact information, for about two years. The drought of new *meishi* made me miss meeting people, especially since there are so many people left to meet in Tokyo.

Before the pandemic, a new *meishi* was clear evidence of entering into a new circle of exchange. I loved that ritual of moving from outside to inside, from not-knowing to knowing, from separate to connected. It's a way of leaping over differences and distances to enter another circle. In Tokyo, it's not what you know, it's whose *meishi* you have.

To be honest, I'm not that much of a schmoozer. But I do exchange *meishi* at jazz clubs, at academic conferences, and with the occasional TV program or publisher, but I'm not a salesman who thrives on *meishi*. In fact, I could live just fine without ever exchanging another one.

But I enjoy the ritual. There's something intriguing about carrying someone's contact data home in your pocket, even if you never use it.

Meishi is a very old ritual, a remnant of when it was impossible to reconnect unless you had some paper record of contact, back when phones were fixed to a wire, and maps were on paper. Like a lot of rituals in Japan, it has staying power. And like many seemingly small things in Japan, it took me a while to master the polite phrases, the correct manner of giving and receiving a card, the subtleties of lingering over a card and making some small, nice comment. It's not just a card, it's an intricate series of gestures.

I've learned to leave the giver's card on the table in front of me (careful to avoid the wet spot from my drink). Having it there is a helpful reminder about the new person's name, affiliation, and position, which are easy to stumble over. I've also learned when and how to place the new *meishi* in my name card holder. Putting it away too soon would be as rude as checking your watch impatiently. Jamming it into a crammed-full wallet would ruin the new relationship by disrespecting the integrity of the card and all it represents.

Japanese judge Japaneseness by these small, subtle details and seem to reset expectations based on performance. It's no different from a hearty handclasp, the Western handshake, which can tell a lot about the person. But *meishi* is a handshake you can take home with you.

All employers print *meishi* for their employees, but I never take the ones from my university. I miss out on the official university logo and font, but I like to get mine special-made on Japanese paper. It's nicer looking and feels better in your hand. There are *meishi* printing shops all over the city, and I've been going to the same one for years. They keep my data on file. I buy them in batches of 300 or so.

Deciding on the *meishi* printing is a project in itself. The shopkeeper pulls out books with paper samples, one-sided or two-sided, colored, thick, thin, western, Japanese. We go over the font for English and for Japanese, the positioning of the letters, and discuss the ink. It takes a week or so to print them, after which I pick them up in person and check them carefully. You can do all that cheaper and quicker online these days, but the old-style shop feels like part of the larger ritual.

I keep my *meishi* in five different places: my university office, my day-to-day bag, the camera case I take to jazz clubs, my home office, and my wallet. I have a special soft-leather wallet—or wallets, I should say since I have three. I keep the office *meishi* in hard plastic cases from the printer, as no one would ever see those, and I always tuck a couple inside my wallet for unexpected situations.

The *meishi* I receive I keep in cigar boxes, I hate to confess. I have different ones for academics, jazz people, friends, and shops or services. Every so often, I organize them. Or I used to. Once, I bought a special *meishi* scanner and a computer program to keep track of them, but email and the internet have swept away even that. But technology will never be as beautiful, human, or succinct and straightforward as the physical object, so I still love the feel of the paper in my hand.

I like to jot down notes on the back to remind myself of the details about that person. If I haven't gotten back in touch or saved their info in my computer address book, I can forget who it was after a while. I like to be able to say, "I'm glad I ran into you," or "How's your new job?" or "Let's meet again." It's a mnemonic of that moment of initial contact. It's a return ticket to that person's world.

I even have *meishi* from shop clerks at department stores, the electrical appliance store, restaurant maitre d's, clothes repair people, and anyone who provides a service or has information I might later need. Shops and restaurants have them too, though fewer now that QR codes, links, apps, and other digital shorthand have taken over. Technological convenience makes sense, but artifacts from the in-person world, *meishi,* cast a stronger spell on me.

More than that, the handing-over ritual serves as a magical transformation from being just one more person in a vast city overflowing with people to an individual with an address, a job, and a place in the world. It locates me in the dense nexus of Tokyo's complex culture, where it's easy to get lost. I *meishi*, therefore I am.

If I meet any of my former students after graduation, they always love to hand me their *meishi*. They pass it over with a gleam in their eye, marking their transition from student to *shakaijin*, a regular member of society. They bow and smile as they pass over that card, completing their student life even more completely than receiving a diploma.

Somehow, *meishi* always look to the future, holding a promise to return, to reconnect, to engage again. In that sense, *meishi* seem to be a talisman for relations, a two-dimensional expression of potential. Maybe not quite a marriage certificate, or an official *jirei* job appointment, they are a miniature record of connection. Meeting people can be an achievement in Tokyo and deserves some written notice.

I'm always intrigued that not only do I have a lot of *meishi* in my collection, but my *meishi* is in other people's cigar boxes or whatever they use as storage. For all those I received, I've given an equal number away, now in the filing system of people all over the city. I wonder about the *meishi* I've handed out, where they've traveled, where they're filed. Do the receivers ever think of me? Maybe not. Maybe they threw mine out, but I'd guess most people hang on to them like I do.

Mostly, of course, the *meishi* just sit on my shelves in my cigar box filing system. I'm sure Marie Kondo would advise me to throw them all out, but frankly, the *meishi* spark joy for me. I love having met those people and having a record of interaction and connection. It chips away at the anonymity of the city and connects the dots—of people and places and their people and places—you didn't even know were there.

One of the ironies of Tokyo is that it's so full of people you can go for weeks—or a year and a half—and not meet anyone new. You're surrounded by people and yet you don't really know them at all. *Meishi*, though, are a kind of knowing, a feeling of not being isolated. I suppose that's an illusion in some ways, just *tatemae* (superficial politeness). But during the pandemic, I missed even that illusion.

After the pandemic eased, I wondered if the *meishi* exchange ritual would return. It did, but not with the previous force of necessity and expectation. It wasn't forgotten like some parts of pre-COVID life. I still had a couple of boxes of *meishi* ready and waiting to be exchanged once again. As life returned to normal, I started reloading my name card wallet. They're a Tokyo necessity if you want a glimpse into other lives and relish the little paper souvenir to remember them with.

Beauty Blossoming

Every year in March and April, everyone in Japan stops to look at the same thing. It's the only time of the year that happens. Usually, people's lives run in diverse ways, but at cherry blossom season, everyone looks in the same direction.

Recently, I walked through Shinjuku Gyoen Park, famed for its cherry blossoms. Even on a cloudy, windy afternoon, the elegant walkways were packed. Lovers strolled, old friends chatted, kids skipped and laughed, colleagues joked and nodded, and everyone posed and took photos, hundreds and hundreds of photos.

It was impossible to find any angle without strangers in the frame. What other flower is so loved that everyone photobombs everyone else? And then shrugs and smiles about it? But maybe we weren't strangers. We were cherry blossom lovers united. We entered other people's photos, and they entered ours.

Cherry trees are popular, but not in the way of some corporate ad campaign for the newest, latest product—they are naturally popular. Like rice, like a smile, like sunlight, they have a natural appeal that needs no promotion. Cherry trees are their own perennial promo feed, advertising only themselves.

Maybe one reason people love cherry trees is because they seem so alive. They're different from too-tall pines or majestic cedars, which command awe and respect, or even smaller blossoming trees, which are necessary and admirable enough. Cherry trees feel closer. The heavy, creaky branches hang down to the earth to meet humanity halfway, like a warm handshake from an old friend.

Cherry trees look best set against other trees and, for a month or more, dominate all other trees. The colors of the blossoms set off all shades of greens and every hue of the sky. They match everything. Those other plants fade into the background while the cherry trees deliver their annual center-stage soliloquy. They draw admirers like a magnet. For a month or more, you rarely see a lonely tree. People crowd around them wherever they are.

Even an old cinderblock wall or a dusty schoolyard is transformed by a single cherry tree. They transform blacktop or plain old dirt into something magnificent, dropping their petals like a comforting shawl over the world's shoulders. People will stop in front of a single tree for a few minutes on their way home, even if they would never stop there any other time of the year. They get us to pause from the rush of our lives and sink into the beauty.

Cherry trees next to rivers, canals, or moats are especially appealing. Fortunately, Japan has plenty of waterways through its cities. The small petals float on top of the surface and turn the water into a long, flowing robe of white and pink. It's no coincidence that flower girls mimic the cherry trees' petal scattering at weddings. Cherry blossom season is the annual wedding of humans and beauty. Not every tree gets its own party, but cherry trees do—every year. And everyone comes.

At night, during cherry blossom season, people carry food and drink to tarps and blankets spread on the ground, and they have *hanami* parties. Spaces are limited, so traditionally, the youngest employees in companies spend their days staking out the best spots for when the other employees come later in the day. Before COVID, the parties could be raucous, a time to really let loose. If you arrive too late, finding a spot is impossible, even if it rains. They're all filled with red-faced drinkers and carried-in feasts.

But I like the daytime better. You can see the full glory of the trees and I love watching people taking photos of others as they nestle themselves against the blossoms, burying themselves in their beauty. I noticed an older woman with a cane brushing her hair and preening her outfit while a friend, or maybe her sister, waited for her to get ready. Like the trees, she was not too old to look good, not too shy to let her beauty show.

Corralled by parents, kids pose for a few seconds before racing off to play tag or ride piggyback with friends or siblings. The photos mark their growth from year to year. Some kids blow soap bubbles, but the bubbles couldn't compete with the petals. The kids know they are supposed to pay attention and appreciate the uniqueness of the cherry trees, which they'll return to for the rest of their lives.

Many foreigners in the park, some perhaps witnessing the spectacle for the first time, hold their camera gear in hand, looking too overwhelmed to know where to start. Their multilingual "wows" continue as their fingers begin pressing the shutter button. They seem to slip into a sort of awed contemplation of what is such a simple, great idea—putting cherry trees all over the place.

I especially love how cherry trees seem to dance. They are always in motion, swaying, hula-ing, shimmying, rising like an ocean wave, making the wind visible for a moment. All trees have their own dance style, but cherry trees have an earthy elegance to theirs. They shake off petals a few at a time, bending and recoiling, their limbs sprightly despite their age.

And people follow suit. Everyone moves differently around the trees. As I looked over the open grounds of the park, everyone's strolling was close to dancing. Women sashay and roll their hips. Men bob their heads and twist their shoulders. People turn to each other, smiling, touching, and gently drifting apart. Everyone sways like dancers in tune with the music of the trees.

People move back and forth in the light, trying to find the best angle to photograph. They search for the right perspective to catch the dappled whites and pinks shifting from glossy to matte to electric. When the sunlight hits them, the color can be almost painful. People seem to be pleading with their cameras to work better to catch all the beauty possible.

The beauty pulls people away from constantly checking their phones. Yes, they check the last photo to make the next one better, but they connect the trees to something deep inside themselves, letting the surface of emails, messages, and online searches disappear for a while. The blossoms are like the opposite of what pops up on a smartphone screen—not just ad-free, but open, natural, and authentic.

That always makes me wonder if there is such a thing as universal beauty, something that all humans can agree on. A glance around suggests everyone has their own taste in what looks good in clothes. But they all agree on the blossoms. And in response, they dress nicely, in neat outfits carefully chosen to do their best next to the beauty of the cherry trees.

And even among the trees, they flock to the more

impressive ones like birds to a feeder, wiggling as close as they can, like carp to crumbs tossed in a pond. There is no hope of getting an individual shot near the prettiest, fullest trees. No angle allows just one person and the tree. There are always too many people.

And in front of the most resplendent trees, people always take extra time to prepare. They don't want to look sloppy when the background is so spectacular. Those taking the photos do so more carefully too. They squint at their screens and position the shot like cinematographers.

Standing there in the act of photographing a fully blossoming cherry tree, it's as if, for a moment, everyone touches the most sublime beauty. We feed off it. We want to take a photo with *that*, to wrap ourselves in it, and exist for a moment, beneath the branches, and in the photograph forever.

And when, at last, we have to leave the trees, we console ourselves that next year, we can again stand in front of the cherry trees to replenish our supply of beauty and recharge our senses to last another year.

Blossoms and Stone

In late March and early April, going out to see cherry blossoms is an obligation that everyone in Japan relishes. It's one of the most agreed-upon customs, one of the most collective urges I know of. Newspapers, magazines, and websites publish a "maximum blossom" estimate up and down the archipelago. Everyone plans the best day carefully because one windy, rainy day can dash all plans. "Hope you got out to see some blossoms" is included in every email and text message.

I try to plan carefully too, because even with good weather, the blossoms are gone before you know it. As a symbol of life's brevity and transience, they arrive as advertised, disappearing quickly. Go for a walk without your camera one day, and you'll miss the peak picture.

After a year of bad news, hibernation, and worrying about the pandemic, the blossoms felt more urgently beautiful than ever. The pandemic broke up the usual blossom-viewing activities but made everyone appreciate them all the more.

The blossoms became a booster shot for beauty, a visual injection of aesthetic energy that re-charges that side of our humanity, vaccinating us against the ugliness of much of the year. It's like a new pair of eyeglasses that lets you see deeply into the delicacy of a single blossom and broadly into the passing of the years.

Maybe I felt that way because I take my annual aesthetic check-up at the cemetery near my house. It's just as important as a health check-up. The cherry blossoms in the cemetery are stunning, their poignancy sharpened by the vast grounds. The land is flat, with wide roads and walkways, endless graves, and lots of sky and no skyscrapers. You can see the trees from far away and up close. It's open enough that the sun can find its way in to sharpen the reds and pinks to nearly purple against the blue sky and to deepen the browns and blacks of the shadowed, craggy trunks.

A cemetery might seem an odd place to appreciate the cherry trees at their best, but all cherry blossoms are viewed in context. Ueno Park is famed for the trees that frame the museums and shelter the temples. Chidorigafuchi's famed trees spill down the bank to the moat around the Imperial Palace. All through Tokyo, cherry trees line walkways, canals, and roads. And always, everywhere, you see the trees with people below, people and blossoms in every frame.

The cherry blossoms in the cemetery near my home are mainly set against graves. The contrast of stone below and flower above always strikes me with melancholy and joy in equal measures. After all, the word for cemetery in Japanese is a two-*kanji* combination of the characters for "soul" and "garden," a delicate balance of the natural and the human, of the linear and the cyclical. You can't help but look at the blossoms without a metaphoric thought or two.

Suffering the second year that *hanami* parties were prohibited because of COVID-19, the two years when they were needed the most, brought back the many times I'd gone in the past. I marveled at the *hanami* parties when I first came to Tokyo. I was a bit wilder then, and boozing in a big group still held a strong appeal. Those parties seemed the epitome of a socializing culture obsessed with relationships, and I liked that then. Now, I can take it or leave it. The blossoms remain.

Every year, I went with groups of friends, students, and colleagues to eat, drink, and talk under the blossoms. One group of writers would gather in Aoyama Cemetery in the section reserved for long-buried foreigners, and we'd party right there as if staking out our future turf and laughing about it.

No parties have ever been allowed in the cemetery near my home in the western plains of Tokyo. It's the kind of place where you automatically lower your voice and look away from other visitors. You can go there for a solitary walk and a long conversation, but the slightest rowdiness wouldn't fit. The quietude alone makes you see the cherry blossoms differently.

The cherry trees in the cemetery seem to be giving quiet solace to the deceased and the grieving, as well as to the passersby like me, who don't know a soul in the place. The branches hang down like a pat on the back. It's hard not to personify them. The branches appear like the fingers of a Buddha or Boddhisatva, a mudra hand gesture towards the earth for patience and compassion, or some other virtue too subtle for me to grasp.

The cherry trees in the cemetery are less trimmed than other blossom-viewing sites because they don't need to be. They have room to spread out like clouds that came down for a lazy visit. And while I'm a materialist when it comes to death, I wouldn't mind an old cherry tree leaning over my final resting spot, its bark as rough as any living thing in old age, its blossoms the flickering white-pink-red of a baby crying.

Throughout the cemetery, individual plots are

delineated by section with numbered markers, all of them distinct and separate from the surrounding plots. It's an ordered, earthly universe until the cherry trees toss their petals all around, more of them than you'd think a tree could produce. The cherry trees line some roads but also pop up randomly here and there, disrupting the burial grid by showering it in random swaths of intense color.

I often stop and look at the names, dates, and epitaphs carved into stone. I like to marvel at the trees and flowering bushes that decorate the interior of the small family plots. Some plots have run to wild abandon, unkempt and neglected, but almost all are spectacularly neat eulogies of polished marble and trimmed plants. I always try to puzzle out the lives that led there. But at cherry blossom time, I rarely stop. The cherry trees keep me moving.

The contrast of the primly placed, sharply hewed stone blocks with the cherry trees is striking. The blossoms are frail and sheer, moving and flowing, almost flying, while the hard, heavy stonework that hunkers around the grey tombs is set, never to move. The blossoms flutter down into piles that form a carpeted path between the rectangles of the raised plots, landing on the stones and rocks like unpredictable punctuation, pink on grey.

Unlike the order inside the plots, the gently swaying limbs of the cherry trees, bright with color, arch up high and wide over multiple graves, stretching out in capricious directions, visually gathering the separate plots into a shared vision of heaven. They make the garden of souls come alive with color and feeling, and make me come alive with the contemplation of the complexity of existence before heading home.

The New Year of April and May

When the cherry blossoms bloom in late March, the entirety of Tokyo seems to bloom with them. Tokyo is at its best from the first rain showers bringing the pure, clean smell of spring until the end of Golden Week through mid-May. Like the plants coming alive in shades of green, yellow, red, and vivid white, Tokyoites also seem to come alive.

From January to late March, it's as if everything is on hold, waiting for the first warm day, the first cherry blossom, the first new spring promise. Then Tokyoites "bloom" with just-bought bags, updated smartphones, and fresh haircuts. New students and workers sport new outfits. People walk with an extra spring in their step and dawdle more too. Life opens to fresh possibilities, and the city hums with energy. There is as much optimism in the air as pollen. It's like a second new year, only warmer, brighter, and richer.

All around the city, mothers take their children to school, gossiping in fresh-pressed suits of similarly dressed mothers. Their children's uniforms glow. Businesspeople eagerly search websites for new places to meet friends or share a drink or a meal. Students stand together in groups, pulling nervously on their hair, exchanging phone numbers, or deciding about their very first *nomikai* drinking party.

By late May, though, Tokyo's flowers have wilted, and so have most people. The famous poet T.S. Eliot said, "April is the cruelest month," but in Tokyo, May is the cruelest month, breeding lethargy and anxiety out of spring beauty.

It is always surprising and depressing when all that April energy collapses under the weight of *gogatsubyo*, literally "May sickness." It's a kind of reluctance and a retreat that descends on Tokyo in May like a psychological typhoon. Every year, after the early May Golden Week holidays, everyone collectively remembers the long lists of obligations, worries, and daily hassles that went unheeded during April. Reality sets in. The fun of the first act of the work and school year turns into the conflicts and contradictions of the year's second act.

Gogatsubyo in late May is the hangover from the high of early spring. The entire city starts to sag. Absences from school and work increase, and everyone hangs their heads on the train. Tokyoites enter a sullen, collective inertia. My students, attentive and enthusiastic for the first four weeks of classes, suddenly look stricken at the assignments, lectures, and presentations that seemed so much fun at first. "This looks interesting" morphs into "I can't do all this." Tokyoites start anxiously confronting the long summer of hard work in front of them.

I always think *gogatsubyo* is a bit strange because nothing like that happens in January after the New Year holidays. There is no "February sickness" even though the Tokyo year really has two starting points: January 1st and April 1st. The starting lines could not be more different.

The official year's start on January 1st feels dark, closed in, and interior. It is steeped in the past. People go to old temples, visit with family, and mull over the past year. It's the introspective side of Japanese culture, a bit melancholy, full of reminders of the passing of time. The new year becomes a time to brood over the past and consider how short the days to come will be.

April 1st is not April Fool's Day here, but it is all go-go, rah-rah excitement. It is optimistic and outgoing, enjoying the present moment and looking forward to better things to come. The warm, pleasant weather pulls Tokyoites out of their mental hibernation and gives them a shot of optimism. Bad moods are shucked off and put away with the heavy winter clothes. Like with any shot, though, too much can be debilitating.

Perhaps there is no downswing after January 1st because January is already depressing, with cold days, early sunsets and the feeling that life is on hold. People stay safe inside, physically and mentally. The euphoria of April drags people out into the sun, so Tokyoites become exposed. Their outgoing side has to present itself, or they must fake it, since everyone else seems so bouncy.

Once April's carefree energy and bubbly enthusiasm wears off, reality reasserts itself, like a train ride home from Disneyland. The serious side of life returns with shocking inevitability. Deadlines, reports, decisions, meetings, and assignments loom ominously. And they all have to be accomplished with the wilting force of the summer's humidity. It's the clean-up after enjoying the party from April to mid-May.

But what startles me every year is how predictable it is. Are the same forces or the same weather conditions pressing everyone at the same time? Is it a kind of infection, like the flu season? My students even use it as an excuse. "Oh, everyone seems so tired," they'll say, explaining a late assignment.

Or maybe it's that Tokyo is a moody place. People fall into moods that others pick up on, or have stored in their annual calendars like birthdays. Don't forget to be in a bad mood after your Golden Week holiday, sometime in mid-May.

Or perhaps I've never gotten over my mental scheduling. May was when school finished in America, so it was an upbeat look to the fun of the summer. I loved May because it was an opening, not a burdening. However, in Tokyo, duties and obligations can be ignored with the enthusiasm of April through the Golden Week in the first week of May. But then it all comes due. The city bends its head on the train under the weight of it all.

The difference between January New Year and April New Year is also partially the old divide in Japanese culture between tradition and modernity. I can never decide which one feels the most Japanese. Is the introverted darkness of January the basic Japanese character? Or are Japanese really the blossom-loving social butterflies of April? January feels like it must have two hundred years ago, but April always seems to look to the future. Which is the real Japanese character? May is when the conflict comes to a head.

I do agree that the distance from May to August holidays seems like a long stretch. If all the good times could be spread out throughout the year, it would be better. If there were "snow viewing parties" in January, not "Golden Week," but "Copper Week" in February, *gogatsubyo* might disappear. "Silver Week" is a new custom in September, and it provides salve for most students and workers, but it's not nearly enough.

Or maybe it's just that people run out of energy, pure and simple. Tokyo's ways of working, studying, playing, and living can be draining. It's as if the entire city runs when it runs and then drops to the side of the marathon at certain points. People sprint when they could pace themselves. When the fun's packed into a week or so, it can leave one (everyone) without the energy to keep going. Maybe by enjoying themselves more all around the year, instead of only at the pre-scheduled, accepted times, Tokyoites could build stamina for enjoying their lives all year round.

But then, what would be the fun of that? There's a pleasure in the melodrama of collapse, real or imagined. Downtime is the one thing Tokyo never has enough of, so it has to be wrestled from the frantic pressures of a city that starts the year twice, not always with the energy needed to act the part.

Summer's Divide

In summer, Tokyo splits in two. Only when summer ends does Tokyo finally come back together as a whole again. This vast urban division isn't economic, political, geographic, or social—it's thermal. In June, the city divides into two completely different spaces—shiver-inducing cold or brain-stunning hot.

Every city in the world takes defensive measures against heat, but Tokyo surely has more air-conditioned spaces than any city in the world. Through the summer, it is like Tokyo has two entirely different seasons—one inside and the other outside. American cities are designed around cars, and Italian cities around churches, but Tokyo seems designed around air conditioning.

The heat is, as is often said, less of an issue than the humidity. When I first moved to Tokyo, it was July, and I was subletting a small apartment with a thermometer and hygrometer hung on the back porch. The thermometer worked fine, up to mid-30 degrees (85 degrees Fahrenheit) and back down after sunset. But the hygrometer was broken. It tilted over the 100% mark day and night. No big deal. It was a cheap one. I tapped on it and changed the batteries to no avail.

Until October, when the hygrometer gently slid back down to 80% and finally, to my relief, down to 60 and even 50%. It wasn't broken at all. Tokyo's humidity stayed that high all summer. High air conditioning served more like a body drying mechanism. You sweated away outside, then got blasted cold-dry inside. Those shifts happened all through the day. Walk to the train and sweat. Get on the train and dry.

I wondered if all those temperature shifts on an average summer day in Tokyo were some Asian health technique, like the cold-water bath after a scalding soak at an *onsen* hot springs bath. Does going back and forth from freezing in stores to sweating on the sidewalk improve blood circulation? Was there some embarrassment to being overheated that overcooling reset?

I couldn't figure it out, but I quickly realized that Tokyo's hot spaces were indeed embarrassing. People pluck their sweaty clothing away from their skin and wipe their faces with goofy little towels. They fan themselves with cheap plastic fold-up hand fans. So, it always feels like it is politeness that keeps thermostats cranked low. Casually mention it is hot outside to a taxi driver, and they will immediately turn the cold knob to high inside.

My summer commute to school puts me through a global tour of climate zones. It's "temperate" at home, "tropical" biking to the station, "subarctic" on the train, "tropical" again from station to school. Then inside my classroom, it's either "polar" (air conditioning fully on in small seminar rooms) or "sub-tropical" (air conditioning half on in lecture halls). I feel sorry for my body having to constantly re-adjust. Or rather, failing to adjust.

Tokyo needs two summer weather reports. The inside weather report would announce the average cold in, say, department stores, subway lines, and *kissaten* coffee shops. Digital maps of Tokyo would be marked for temperature, as they are for traffic, and would tell people how to get from here to there without walking outside in the heat. With that kind of map in hand, some Tokyoites might never go outside all summer. Some transportation apps do show ways to walk inside out of the rain, but humidity is harder to avoid.

Japanese always claim to love harmony, but temperature is one issue on which no one ever agrees. Students turn the air conditioning on. I turn it off. Or I turn it on, and they turn it off. Women wearing short skirts turn it down. My hulking western body clamors for cool. At meetings, the older professors crank the thermostat to the lowest setting and pour themselves hot tea. The younger professors suffer in silence. Everyone wears wildly different layers and thicknesses of clothing. Like some game of musical temperature chairs, someone is always left out of their comfort zone.

The temperature segregation of Tokyo summer always makes me wonder about the city's true nature. Which is the real Tokyo—the cool artificially controlled spaces or the sweltering natural environment? My answer changes from day to day through the humid summer months. Some days, I wonder why anyone would be foolish enough to build a major world city in such a tortuous summer climate. On other days, I embrace the heat and try to endure it with cold beer and well-placed fans.

In summer, strangely, Tokyo's cold spaces start to feel the most natural, even though they are the most artificially created. Are people truly themselves only when they are unnaturally comfortable? If you're "comfortable," shouldn't that be natural? Tokyoites can stand dense crowds, high prices, long commutes, and small living spaces, but they cannot stand to shop, sit, or walk in a temperature too far from "normal."

The drive for comfort in whatever form is part of what

makes Tokyo Tokyo. The idea that comfort can be provided, manufactured, or constructed is essential to the urban environment. The idea that a city does not even need to pretend to be "natural" is basic as well. This tenet of Tokyo life gives it a science fiction feel. One day, sending a friend off, I traveled from home to the station, to other trains to the airport, and home again without going outside. I remained constantly inside. And therefore, reasonably comfortable.

This Tokyo penchant for controlling the surrounding environment is an odd contrast with the traditional love of nature inherent to Japanese art, gardens, architectural design, and the inclusion of nature in even small pockets of life with flower arrangements or bonsai. Or maybe all of those cultural expressions are another way of molding and shaping nature into a human conception, making it easy on the eye, relaxing to the body, or comforting to the mind.

Tokyo's drive for comfortably cool interior spaces is a big project. And in my estimation, it doesn't always work, especially with air conditioning. The shift is one thing, the destruction of resources another. Can't shoppers occasionally be discomforted as they move through department stores? Can't commuters take a moment to wipe off a little sweat or fan themselves? The summer rage for a couple of years in a row has been a handheld battery-powered fan. For me, a bit of heat and sweat throughout the day makes the cool of a beer in the evening taste much better.

More than changing geography by diverting a river or defying gravity by building a skyscraper, Tokyo wants to tame the very air to provide comfort for humans. Why not just throw a bubble over the entire city and cool the whole thing? I sometimes wonder. Perhaps that's next? Tokyo—the refrigerated city.

With electricity-saving campaigns increasingly popular, people might have to change their expectations and get used to not being fully chilled all summer. The environment can't support being modified that fully and completely. Even still, the day at the end of the summer when the outside temperature cools, and the city's air-conditioning infrastructure relaxes, comes as a relief. I call it "temperature equinox day."

On that day, the city once again feels balanced and whole as Tokyoites return to thoughts other than just the weather and what it does to them.

Sudden Fireworks

While lying down on the sofa to read, sweating in the thick summer night, I heard a sound like drumming in the sky, a kind of organized thunder. Fireworks! Summer was here. The fireworks season had begun.

I thought it might be too far away to see, so I lolled around on the sofa with my book, enjoying the sound, wondering where it came from: the stadium, the racetrack, or a far river park, all ten-minute bike rides away.

But as the fireworks continued, I crawled off the couch and climbed to the second floor to peer out from my balcony. Maybe I could catch a glimpse. I waited, and in a few seconds, a white flame shot over the tops of the trees. Perhaps it wasn't that far, but the angle was wrong. I went back downstairs, out the front door, and down to the end of my street.

A small crowd had gathered at the top of a pedestrian slope leading down to the park. Large cherry trees used to line the steep slope, but a few years ago, a power line construction project necessitated cutting down most of the cherry trees. Everyone was outraged, but they were replanted. The new trees were still braced in place, not yet grown too tall to see over.

Standing in the humidity was a fair collection of people. Kids in post-bath loungewear raced around, climbing up on their parents' shoulders, anticipating the next ka-pow and ooh and ahh. I didn't look at them much because the shell launches started speeding up, popping higher, tumbling over each other, tattooing the sky. Whatever our age, we squealed in awe and delight, disappointed only to have missed the perfect photo.

The week before, I'd been too busy to read the local newspaper, so the pop-pop-pop came as a surprise. The sound and sight of fireworks, like the buzz of cicadas and the whir of fans, are quintessential to Japanese summer. But even nicer is having them near where you live, unexpectedly. It makes you feel rich, like owning a place within earshot of the ocean or with a picture-window view of Mount Fuji.

Unlike in the U.S., where I grew up, fireworks in Japan are not limited to one single day. Strangely, that seems to make them more special, not less. On the Fourth of July in my hometown of Kansas City, fireworks were a big part of mid-summer. It was a day we could be a little wild, a little dangerous, blowing things up and shooting stuff into the sky.

But that was always just one day. Japanese fireworks are spread out over the summer. They were common in Japan long before 1776 was even a glint in the revolutionary American eye. They celebrate independence in the States but form part of the long-lingering beauty of summer in Japan.

That evening was the Tanabata Festival, a holiday celebrating the meeting of two mythical lovers on the seventh day of the seventh lunar month when their two stars align. That upped the romance level. But in Japan, almost any summer-y thing could serve as reason for a local display. In the Tokyo-Yokohama area, you could practically see fireworks once a week during the hottest summer months.

I've been to most of the biggest annual fireworks

displays in Japan. I loved watching the Kamakura fireworks from the beach. The reflection off the water was doubly spectacular. The Sumida River Fireworks, which one million people recently attended for the first time in four years, are the most famous and longest running. But they require walking a long way or waiting in line to get on a crowded train, not to mention preparing bug spray, hand fans, drinks, light clothing, the works.

Outside your home is less an outing than an effortless comfort. Standing in the dark with my neighbors, almost none of whom I knew, still felt neighborly. We could see the fireworks rise above the tree line. We couldn't see the initial upward thrust, but once it cleared the treetops, the full bright burst was magnificent, more so with the extra seconds of unseen suspense.

The pop-zing-pop-silence emerged from the constant drone of cicadas like a jazz solo. As each one rose in the sky, it gave me the illusion the fireworks were emerging from the trees, art arising out of nature. Trees stay, but fireworks vanish in seconds—the beauty of endurance versus the beauty of the moment, two aesthetic positions side by side.

More neighbors gathered at the viewing spot and joined the chorus of wows and giggles. We were all kids stretching our necks to follow one or two of the shimmering, lingering rockets. Some kids had not seen fireworks for the last few years, maybe at all, because of the pandemic. Their exclamatory questions bounced around the adult ears like whispers of summer mysteries to come.

With a child's eyes, the colors seemed more fun. Adapting between dark and light, it was hard to fully take in all the colors flipping so fast from white yellow to neon green, electric red to teal, turquoise, and violet. Colors went by too fast to identify, remember, or think more than, "I liked that one," before they succumbed to gravity, dribbling, twinkling, and glittering back to earth.

The internet tells me it's barium green, copper blue, strontium red, sodium yellow, and a mix of titanium, zirconium, and magnesium for silvery white. One can imagine the sophisticated construction of the shell, the chemical combinations, and the tricks to set the precisely timed bursts, but it hardly matters. Fireworks are one of those things where knowing the science doesn't add much. More than a technological miracle, they are a celebration of the unpredictable. It's an aerial application of color to the most enormous canvas of all—the night sky.

Fireworks seem more primal than other cultural expressions. Maybe it's the redirection of gunpowder from its usual horrible purposes into something so overwhelmingly beautiful. One wonders, as always, why technology so often goes wrong, and the beautiful side loses out. Fireworks are when the good guys win, for once, when technology faithfully serves creativity, joy, and pleasure. It's when technology delights purely.

A week later, just after sunset, I heard the same rumble and pop from the other direction outside my house. I rushed upstairs, looked out the second-floor window, and saw them—again—even more clearly, though farther away. The family across the street was leaning out their window too. We waved.

It was then that I remembered that in old Edo times, fireworks were shot up as an homage to the victims of famine and disease and as a ritual to drive away future famine and disease. I can understand that. After canceling fireworks for three or four years, it seemed no different now, driving away the pandemic and remembering the lives lost.

Fireworks feel like an echo of something even farther back in human history, the little joy in the pop of a spark from a shared fire in some ancient cave. The cold and fear of the inky night becomes, for a moment, allayed. Night becomes tolerable, safe, and lovely. It's not that fire is the first technology; it's more that fire encapsulates the creative spirit. Fireworks celebrate that spirit as much as any holiday.

Of course, I wasn't thinking about that as I watched the fireworks. I wasn't thinking much at all. I was whispering, "*Sugoi!*" along with everyone else. I was too busy learning again to focus on the successive bursts of life's moments, hoping more are coming, each more amazing than the last.

Tokyo Christmas Trees

After years in Tokyo, friends still ask me if I miss Christmas in America. I don't. Mainly because there's a lot of Christmas in Tokyo. Christmas starts sneaking into Tokyo from the start of December. Within a week or two, glitzy lights, wreaths, Santa hats, window snow, and the whole kit and caboodle of Christmas imagery start invading the city. Western Christmas songs—in English—start pumping out of overhead speakers with gooey, echoey insistence.

Even after I arrive at the calming quiet of my station's bicycle parking lot, a single rooftop reindeer made of wire and lights and a motor that turns its head back and forth watches me creepily as I retrieve my bike from the parking lot. Bad taste knows no borders, I think, and then ride into my relatively undecorated neighborhood, passing only a few lights on homes as I go.

I'm not Scrooge-ish or Grinch-like, but the jarring compulsion to copy Christmas works overtime in Tokyo. Stores and streets are at their most intensely un-Tokyo-like during December. I resolve to surf any wave of good feeling, be it silly, tacky, or tasteless, but every year, it's an effort to forgive the cheery advertising impulse of Tokyo. It surrounds you like in other countries but confuses you too, with its foreignness.

Most people don't think about the Christmas decorations, know their meaning, or care. They look nice, and they change the atmosphere and look of the city. That's enough. It's not that everyone becomes Christian or does much on Christmas. It's a workday like any other.

The secular side of Christmas involves plenty of shopping, and few countries do consumerism better than Japan. Stores, walkways, and advertisements are festooned with whatever Christmas imagery can be packed in. It's not just to make money, though. Tokyo loves dressing up in anything, so draping itself in silver tinsel, fir trees, fake frost, and cotton snow is just one more costume in the yearlong cosplay.

The most common image among those adorning the city is undoubtedly the Christmas tree. They are everywhere: in videos, on signboards, in front of restaurants, popping up like glittering green mushrooms in the most unexpected places—along with all the expected ones. Fir and spruce trees show up throughout the history of Japanese art, from energetic dashes of *sumi-e* black ink to tastefully shaped bonsai trees, but Christmas trees seem more Disney than Zen.

What Tokyo plops down in front of everything from convenience stores to yakitori shops to apartment lobbies look more like upside-down triangles school kids made with blunt-tip scissors and green craft paper. Most of the trees are colored a green so synthetic it de-naturalizes everything around it. The faux trees and tree decorations are no doubt paid for with petty cash doled out by harried store managers and arranged by part-timers like an obligation to cheer up otherwise dead spaces.

Nor do the Christmas trees reflect anything of their closest Japanese equivalent—the genuinely lovely *kadomatsu*, a stately New Year decoration of pine branches set on either side of a home gate or business door, purifying and honoring all who pass between them. Trimmed with bamboo, plum tree sprigs, and circles of rice stalks, they are striking and solemn. They are not brightly lit, so they keep their shadows. They signal a passing through, an entering, rather than the stretching upward of a western tree. When I start seeing these, I know Christmas tree season will soon end.

And yet, I sympathize with the aesthetic impulse to nicen up dull spaces. I can see why stores, restaurants, and offices want to liven things up before the next year arrives. Like them or not, and I'm a bit of both, they are celebratory baubles that soothe the anxiety, fatigue, and dull routine that piles up like dirty shoveled snow at the end of the year.

Still, I can't see why the trees are so common in Tokyo. Most parts of Christmas already have a counterpart in Japanese culture. There's gift-giving, family gathering, spiritual recalibration, and shopping galore, all of which are already well rooted. And there is constant celebration. December is *bonenkai* season for year-end parties and get-togethers. And yet, Tokyoites crave a bridge to other experiences, values, and ways of spending time. The Christmas trees always seem like a longing for something else

Is there something missing from those celebrations that the trees make up for? Why import something new? Why not rework what's already there? But apparently, before the year finishes, the mimetic compulsion for something non-Japanese asserts itself. Maybe Tokyoites just need a different cheerleading squad to rouse the crowd at the final game of the season.

When I see those trees, I feel that Japan is an island nation, an isolated archipelago, as the Japanese point out. But it doesn't seem to be isolated at Christmas time. The trees seem like a way of looking at other cultures a bit wistfully, maybe hungry for connection, for some similar experience, as if the experience here is not enough. To fill in the blanks, Tokyo needs Christmas, or whatever they imagine Christmas to be.

Oddly, too, Christmas is a day for lovers in Japan. Hotels (regular hotels and love hotels) are always solidly booked for couples. Hotels offer lavish overnight dinners, champagne, and room packages, all with a night view of the city. To be young and not have a date on Christmas is a bit embarrassing. My students gossip, moan, or blush about their Christmas plans.

At restaurants, special Christmas set courses are the norm. This always confuses me a bit, as ordering a variety of things and piecing them together is part of the fun of a holiday meal out. However, Christmas is the one night throughout Tokyo where you can never order a la carte. Instead, restaurants compete to assemble the most innovative and striking course meals possible. Reservations are hard to get.

Meanwhile, harried mothers order fried chicken buckets from fast food outlets and have little home parties. Of course, the buckets have Christmas trees on them, as does every fast-food joint. Tokyo kids grow up on Christmas.

Strangely, the Christmas trees strike me as an expression of *mono no aware*, the Japanese aesthetic of "sadness in things." That's usually reserved for less glitzy things, a fallen wet leaf or a rusting bicycle. But the odd placement, unexpected presence, and cheap materiality of Tokyo Christmas trees hit me with a deep melancholy. The trees seem lonely, so far from the land where they originated. They feel so far from their origins, as lost as a tourist on the wrong train.

But then again, who doesn't need another tree or two and a splash of green as the world turns colorlessly winter? I guess I do. I'll admit the trees tickle me.

So, rather than Grinch and Scrooge about it, I focus on the irony of it all and play a little game with myself as I move around the city—I try to find the tree set in the most incongruous place. I keep my eyes open for the place I could never conceive of putting a Christmas tree for any reason whatsoever. I photograph it and put it up on my website and my SNS. Posting sad tree photos gives me seasonal joy. *Look at that one!* I think when I spy one hiding amongst the shelves, blocking an entryway, or jammed in beside sale items on the sidewalk. I let them amuse me as a present to myself.

Whatever oddness the season in Tokyo presents to those who grew up in Christmas-celebrating countries, one thing is for sure: Christmas helps infuse the mundane workday life with a sense of fun and transforms the bleakness of winter into something magical and festive. Who doesn't need that gift?

A Clean Ending

On the last day of the year, my western Tokyo neighborhood fills with the hum of machines and the splash of water. The swish of brooms and the clink of laundry poles echo through the air. Cars get sponged and hosed down. Wet patches spill over the narrow roads where buckets have been emptied to sluice away the year's dirt. The last few days of the year, but especially on the last day, laundry covers the poles and not the usual laundry, but blankets, sofa covers, and futons. Everything washable gets washed. Every surface, inside and out, gets a wash, wipe, or sweep. Everyone is cleaning everything. Even the cleaning equipment gets cleaned—gloves, mops, buckets, and rags.

It's "*Osoji*," or "big cleaning," a ritual of energy and activity that brings the year to a close and leaves everything sparkling clean. It's a clean ending for a clean start.

My neighbor across the road was working on his gutters as I headed off for my last jog of the year. I stopped to offer my New Year greetings. "You're in charge of the outside?" I ask him. He looked in need of the last beer of the year. He had an old vacuum cleaner, a hose, deck brooms, and bags of swept-up leaves, trash, and gunk arrayed around the perimeter of his home.

"It's too busy inside. It's safer out here," he said, nodding at the front door. The angry whir of a vacuum cleaner came from inside. "I don't dare go back in," he added, returning to his task. "*Ganbatte*! Good luck!" I shout.

I head for the park, feeling guilty and a bit smug for not doing any cleaning whatsoever. All I want is a good, solid jog, which I tell myself is a "big cleaning" of my body, pumping out the toxins from the end-of-the-year parties.

The park is neat and clean since the maintenance crews blew all the leaves into piles, scooped them up, and hauled them off. The park is messy only after a big storm or when the crews fall behind, cutting back the summer growth. They usually leave the cherry blossoms scattered, but that hardly needs cleaning. It's part of the design.

When I return from my jog in the park, my other neighbor is bent over his gutter, sweeping up with the same short broom and pan his father used every morning until he died a few years ago. His father was, I think, a bit deaf, but I still practiced morning greetings with him, the same every day with a dignified bow when I first came to Tokyo.

"Cleaning up?" I shout to his son, who is now in charge of the front street area. He stands and nods, holding the broom and pan. "It's the last day of the year," he reminds me, the question left hanging whether I've finished my cleaning.

I point at my house like we're working on the inside, but we haven't even started. Appreciating a ritual and following it are two different things. I suppose I've failed to adapt to Japanese cleanliness standards, but so be it. My wife and I haven't done much other than shop and recover from the year. My neighbors all have multiple trash bags filled and ready for the first trash pickup of the year. Extra workers have to be hired for the task.

Of course, every culture has its cleaning rituals, such as spring cleaning, and tricks and customs for keeping one's home safe, tidy, and livable. But I can't help but feel culture shock thinking of the American end of the year, which is more about partying. Yeah, you'd do the dishes, but not that much else. The need to let loose is paramount in America. However, the need for tidiness is the greater force in Japan.

I'm always pressured to clean by stores. The week before New Year, stores set out massive displays of cleaning products—bottles, brooms, towels, sponges, buckets of all descriptions and price ranges. It comes in feeds online. It's such a given, it's everywhere.

I'm always tempted to buy stuff and get into it, and in general, I've become cleaner and more orderly over the years in Japan. It's sunk into my messy mind by osmosis. But I just don't feel any of the moral, aesthetic, or cultural—ritual—pressure to get everything spic and span. My parents were indifferent housekeepers, and I moved too often once I started college to think much about how things looked or felt. I like things to be clean, but I don't feel ashamed when they aren't.

At the end of the year, rather than clean, I still want to unwind, American-style. I don't mind reviewing the year, feeling nostalgic and hopeful for the following year. I relish a few days of downtime to mull over the passing of time, contact old friends, and wonder at the mystery of calendar demarcations and the sweep of the second hand on clocks, digital or otherwise.

But maybe that's what everyone in my neighborhood thinks while cleaning. Perhaps they're feeling the same, but doing things differently. Maybe keeping my hands busy would help stave off regret or despair. I do like things clean.

I run out for a few last-minute items on my bicycle, and down the street, a car has been pulled out of its just-wide-enough parking spot for a full wash and wipe. On the other side of Tokyo, one shrine offers a special talisman secured on the car for divine protection. Putting that on a dirty car would be an insult to the gods and probably wouldn't work.

In offices all over the city, the tradition of everyone in the company—from high to low—cleaning up the office together is as common as going out for *bonenkai* forget-the-year parties. Big cleaning is a sort of forget-the-dirt party, removing last year's symbolic—and actual—dirt so the year can start clean. The compulsion to ensure everything is ready for the transition from one year to the next, from one state—dirty, old, and used—to the next—clean, refreshed, and ready is powerful.

I'm not sure I see the past as something to be dusted. Isn't it something to be cherished just as it is, a bit dirty or messy? I don't want to dispense with all the grit and grime of the past. Some of it seems part of life. The world, the years passing, is not like Disneyland, polished to perfection. People are messy, even at their best.

Or maybe the big cleaning at the end of the year is just another, bigger version of keeping things clean that happens all through the year. In almost no other country than Japan would you find workers holding a rag to the handrail of an escalator in the train station or cleaning an already clean public toilet. In the morning, shopkeepers clean up their part of the sidewalk and ensure the front area looks good before opening, just like my neighbor.

Or maybe there is no division between material and spiritual, as the Western world seems to believe. Maybe cleanliness really is next to godliness. Maybe what's on the outside does reflect what's on the inside.

Over the years, I have come to love this big cleaning ritual, though at a distance. Everything around me—visible or not—is cleaner at the start of the year. It's not just imagined. Storefronts and interiors are spiffed up. My gym's pool is drained, cleaned, and refilled. Cars gleam in the sun. Windows sparkle. The very air of Tokyo feels fresher and purer. And strangely, so do I.

It's a massive effort to get Tokyo to its peak cleanliness. For a few days after New Year's until the first return to work, the city is cleaner than at any other time of the year.

108 Bells

On New Year's Eve in Japan, I step outside into the cold just after midnight to hear the temple bells. The deep, resonant bell tones flow up the hill from a temple on the plains below. The 108 bells, rung one at a time, with silence in between, always give me pause. Listening to them is how I start every year. New Year in Japan is usually quiet, with no Times Square squealing or champagne corks popping.

Temple bells are rung 108 times, once for each of the 108 earthly desires, it is said. I try to count them, desires and bells, but I always lose track and end up sinking into the clear sound in the chill night air. The peacefulness of the bell eases my mind, so my thoughts stray from the count and meander through hope for the new year and memories of the last. In Buddhist belief, those desires cause pain and suffering. Ringing the bell causes those desires to vanish, so the year starts with a fresh, clean heart.

I close the year out with a few friends at most or just eating Chinese dumplings with my wife. We boil up scads of them and survive on them for days. No one cooks the first few days of the year, but we're not Japanese enough to make the traditional *osechi* dishes, and buying a boxed set of those at a department store, as more and more people do, is startlingly expensive. Dumplings are relatively easy to make, boil, eat, and save in the freezer.

The lead-up to the bell ringing is a program shown only once a year on NHK, the public broadcasting station. It only lasts thirty minutes or so, but it's my favorite show of the year. NHK, with its vast resources, sends crews to famous temples all over Japan. From the freezing cold of Hokkaido to the short sleeves of Okinawa, the crews show Japanese lining up to get into temples, hoping to arrive at the front during the first minutes of the year.

Each temple has its own special ceremony, but people usually sit *seiza* with heads bowed as Buddhist priests chant sutras and tap drums in unison. Or they line up waiting for hours to pray at the inner shrine after dropping in coins, ringing a tinkly little bell on a rope, and scattering away to take photos.

Others, though, pay large sums to reserve a spot to ring the big bell. At the same moment, bells all over Japan send out their deep timbre and lingering resonance. The bells are large enough to require a structure made from thick beams of wood set on a raised platform.

One by one, the bell ringers for the year grasp the pull rope attached to a huge clapper hung horizontally from ropes next to the bell. The rope is swung back and forth until the last strike when the clapper whacks the bell and sends out that purifying tone. At some temples, the bell is so large and the clapper so heavy it takes the full weight of a priest or a paid-up penitent to strike the bell strongly enough. The bell in my neighborhood decays with a beautiful, gently lessening tone.

The silences between the rings are just as impressive and meaningful. The bell works its magic, but then the quietude does too. It's the spiritual "ah un" of the life force breathing in and out. It's always moving. Transformative, I would say. Energy is transformed into sound, and sound is transformed into a new mindset.

Whenever I stop by a temple, I take a photo of its large bell. At most temples, you can only ring it on special occasions. Even quiet and unmoving on their towers and platforms, they're impressive. Bells are thought to ward off evil and keep the worst spirits at bay. The sound of the bell is also important to some meditation practices, signaling the moment when meditation stops or a new round of sutras begins.

As a music lover, I also like the neat, tight harmonics. It's like a summary of all the sounds I've listened to throughout the year on speakers, headphones, earbuds, and lives. It's as if a year's worth of music is compressed into the ur-sound of the bell so the next year's music can unfold.

The sound is celestial and otherworldly, a sharp contrast to a ride cymbal in fast-tempo jazz. The bell is rung slowly—the 108 rings take time—creating a massive, slow unfolding of sound that stretches out to hills, valleys, houses, and surrounding areas.

Setting the bell in motion is musical in the grand sense of "the music of the spheres." That old belief that the movement of celestial bodies is like musical relationships starts to make sense when the tone comes through the cold, night air. The proportions, distances, and inter-relations of the physical and musical worlds appear in sync for 108 moments.

The tone of some bells resounds for long distances. The penetrating power has been measured as carrying 32 kilometers or 20 miles on a clear night. That reaches a big audience, everyone listening from their most cherished spots, family homes, back porches, or local temples, all within earshot of the bell. It reminds you how close you are if a bell can unite you.

There's something so gentle about the tolling of the New Year bell. I'm not sure it washes away all my desires, but it does make me feel insignificant in the larger scheme of things. It also reconnects me to things I let slide in the rush of the year, like attention to the beauty and mystery of the world.

I like the peacefulness of the bells. I read that during World War II, the demand for materials like metal was so great that the military decreed that temple bells would be plucked like fruit and melted down to construct the war machinery. I have always liked to imagine that after the war, the reverse happened. The metal used in the war was melted down and returned to the bell shape. I doubt that's true, but I'd like it if it were.

The bells establish peace and reset the attitude toward the coming year, hoping for peace for oneself, those within the sonic range of the temple bell, and, from there, for everyone in the outgoing circles of the world.

After standing in the cold on my back porch, looking up at the stars, and thinking backward and forward until the final bell, I go inside to warm up and somehow carry inside the feeling of the bell and hope it keeps resonating as the year begins.

Part III
Small Intensities

Introduction

Though Tokyoites can appear indifferent or lackadaisical about the city around them, they also relish intense experiences. Small ones, mainly. There are moments when Tokyo life pushes through its restraints and meets people with full force.

I'm not the kind of person who is always seeking out big intense experiences. The small intensities of Tokyo are enough to amaze me. I write about those in this section. These are not necessarily everyday experiences, nor are they rare exploits. They are small happenings that surprised me, but which I found delightful and meaningful.

Tokyo's density of people sharpens and deepens life, which is why people have always gravitated to the city, but it can also overwhelm life. You can miss the trees because the forest is so large. Tokyo often subverts expectations and received notions in marvelous ways. The experiences I write about here mix pleasure with exasperation, amusement, and wonder.

Of course, like anywhere else, Tokyo's daily life has elements of dull routine. But what I find spectacular about Tokyo are the many experiences that break the routine with vigor and ferocity. Some of these are universal or have counterparts in other cities and cultures, but the ones I've chosen for this section all have a uniquely Tokyo flavor.

Japanese culture always presses toward perfection, which makes for the intensity of food, spaces, movement, and feeling. Maybe perfection is Tokyo's way of expressing intensity. There's an element of that in some of these events and happenings. It's not that these things couldn't happen in huge cities other than Tokyo. It's that they didn't. They happened here.

Tokyo's vastness means that you can lose mental direction in the waves of sensory experience. It's easy to miss the small things in your hands or underfoot but noticing and cherishing them makes Tokyo an even more fascinating place.

A Procession of Pottery

Hakone is where Tokyoites go to recover. It's a hilly area an hour and a half west of Tokyo and offers *onsen* hot springs resorts. The bath, the bed, and the bamboo outside the hotel balcony in the afternoon sun were all perfect. Like everyone else, I wanted to relax and unwind for a few days away from everyday hassles.

After soaking, napping, and reading all afternoon, dinner started arriving at 6:45, just as the server said it would when she showed us to our room. I snuggled up to the floor table for the performance. The server carried a tray filled with dishes into our room. She knelt on the tatami and began placing the small dishes one by one onto the table delicately and caringly. One by one, each dish touched down on the wood with a light thunk, like notes in a jazz solo, as the room filled with the aroma of steamed veggies and grilled fish.

There were so many dishes that it took the next two hours to load and unload them all. It was more a stream of pottery than it was a single meal. Some dishes could be eaten in a few bites, others a few more, but the dishes were all a delight to the eyes on the way to the mouth. The beauty of the small dishes enhanced the taste of the food. The neat little dishes were the aesthetic opposite of the plastic wrapping on a convenience store onigiri, which is purely functional.

I once read that the custom of serving food in multiple, small, diverse sizes, shapes, patterns, and colors of pottery started as a way of amusing the daughters of merchants in old Osaka. A wealthy urban family at that time would never cook at home. They'd order out. So, to keep the rich household happy, a succession of ever-unique plates and bowls had to be rotated to keep the family's business.

If that's true, and it sounds true to me, our eighteen-hour stay at the *onsen* felt like a week's worth of different dishes in less than a day.

I became fascinated as I sampled each one, wondering how many dishes had arrived in total. The numbers meant little compared to the beauty, but I counted anyway.

Dinner (6:45)

Hors d'oeuvres 5 (square and round, flat and curved glass)

Hot soup 1 (2 if you count the lid)

Sashimi 2 (one white box and one circular soy sauce/wasabi dipping bowl)

Steamed dish 1 (again, not counting the top)

Fried fish 1

Noodles 1

Baked dish 1 (metal plate in wood frame)

Cold salad 1

Rice, pickles, miso soup 3

Dessert 3 (4 if you count the tray) (5 if you count the gold paper)

Teacup 1

Sake flask and cup 2 (flask refilled twice)

Beer glass 1

Chopstick rest 1

Total: 22

I sat at the table, going through the dishes like photos from a vacation. They were a blur of colors, shapes, and textures as if the chef were trying to include every variation of pottery. I wondered who selected which dish for which item. Was the head chef in charge? Was there a sous-chef just in charge of colors? Who was the culinary designer who matched them all up? It seemed more complex than the interior design of an entire household.

A glass or two of sake dispelled my questions and eased me into the flow of a delicious meal, after which I was ready for another soak in the bath. There's no sleep deeper than after a steamy outdoor bath. Or maybe it was the mesmerizing flow of watching all the dishes arrive, put in place one by one, and then picked up one by one and carted off again. Soaking in the bath, I dreamed of myself steamed like one of the gorgeous items on the menu.

The next morning, the ceremonial parade of pottery began again. Breakfast dishes were harder to count since the server needed two or three deliveries to get them all in place. The various dishes, bowls, pots, plates, dispensers, and containers filled the large, low table.

I wasn't even sure how to count. Should I include the dark orange origami box that held the umeboshi dried-plum pits? Even the discarded parts were set on a lovely receptacle. The curved lacquer containers for *oshibori* (hot hand towels) and the placemats counted too. They seemed as carefully chosen and as delicately placed as at dinner. The actual number didn't matter compared to the striking beauty of the table covered in dishes, but here's the count from the morning:

Breakfast (8:30)

Grapefruit juice glass 1

Eggplant dish 1

Green vegetable dish 1

Western salad 1

Western salad dressing dish 1

Sashimi plate 1

Fish and fish egg bowl 1

Boiled tofu dumpling pot 1
(wood container and fire pot below, and wood top)

Fried fish, egg, and vegetable plate 1

Yoghurt and fruit plate 1

Rice bowl 1

Soy sauce dispenser 1

Soy sauce dipping tray 1

Miso soup bowl 1 (not counting the top)

Toothpick container 1

Umeboshi plum plate 1

Umeboshi plum pit holder 1 (pits only)

Leftover inarizushi container 1 (uneaten midnight snack)

Teapot 1 (shared)

Teacup 1

Teacup saucer 1

Lacquered rice warmer 1 (shared)

Rice scoop bowl (with warm water) 1 (shared)

Extra bowl with spoon (not sure what for) 1

Chopstick rest 1

Total: 25 (more than dinner)

Was this what it was like to be a wealthy merchant in the Edo Period? And who washes all these? If we had those small dishes at home, I'd have to get a teensy dishwashing sponge.

I wondered how the server could remember the order. The cooks may have placed them in order. She placed them in the same spot for both my wife and me, which must have been the correct spot. Was there one particular place that's better for the Western-style salad? Or was she free to improvise?

And where did they store all these serving dishes? They must use a storage system with an intricate network of specially shaped shelves. The place didn't seem big enough to accommodate all the dishes. And what about seasonal dishes? You didn't want too much orange or brown in spring and not too much green or pink in fall. I wondered if we were using one season's dishes.

So, I asked her. She looked at me as if she had never heard that question before. It took me a minute to figure out her explanation, and I thought I had asked some taboo question, as I often embarrassingly do. She replied that a pottery delivery service brought new pottery to match the rotating menu for each season. When we returned, perhaps in the fall (if we could afford it), there would be all new pottery to fit the fall food.

I felt stunned at the detail of this miniature parade, at how well the food matched what held it. Which came first—the food or the dish? The table became a canvas on which to paint with superbly cooked food and artistically selected dishware.

As I thought about the micro-majesty of all the porcelain, lacquerware, and glass we'd been fed from, I felt the steaming hot water working as a fixative, setting the colors and patterns of the food and the dishes deep into my mind, making sure the memory wouldn't run or fade and would remain with me for a very long time.

Tokyo Masked

The apparition of these faces in the crowd:

Petals on a wet, black bough.

"In a Station of the Metro" by Ezra Pound

For about two years, Tokyo became a faceless city. As the pandemic lurched forward, people masked up, making Tokyo the most masked city in the world. But even as remote work returned to regular commuting and meeting, Tokyoites remained masked. As I restarted in-person classes, in-person commutes, and the occasional meal out, I couldn't see faces, one of the most magnificent parts of a city with a fantastic number of faces. They were all hidden.

I'm not against self-protection, public health, or even a slight veiling of the mysteries, but Tokyo Masked was disappointing and confusingly creepy. Everything that made Tokyo a fascinating place—intimate restaurants, teensy stores, standing bars, underground clubs, and the constantly close life—makes Tokyo a great place for virus exchange. If I were a virus, I'd choose Tokyo. But in containing the viral, the beautiful disappeared and was replaced with little squares of white.

As a novelist, I'm an observer of people and have never minded my commutes for just that reason. Public space has always been a place to learn. Watching an overworked salaryman dozing, the determined glare of a student pouring over a study book, and the day-off nonchalance of a young couple shopping were more than observations. They were the opening lines of stories. With everyone masked, I felt cut off not just from other people but from their stories too.

Stories come through the body, through an entire vocabulary of gestures, postures, and motions. Japanese have always excelled at body politeness, especially in public. In Tokyo, polite body language is needed to get by. But that was intensified with everyone masked. In Tokyo's cramped spaces, it was impossible to social distance two meters, but everyone kept their distance however they could. It made everyone tenser and more aware of *mawari no hitotachi*, "the people around," who could be carrying the virus you don't want to have.

It used to be that some women on the train, and men too, would spend a chunk of their commute grooming themselves, putting on make-up, adjusting their hair, checking their bangs. They'd use hand mirrors or cellphone cameras for self-scrutiny or stop by a window or shiny metal surface to give themselves a check. But not with masks on. They couldn't see through them. Rather than meticulously prepping their faces, they covered them. Nothing's left to primp once the masks are roped over the ears.

With the masks themselves, I'd hoped Tokyo would do its usual thing and start juicing up the design. But that didn't happen. I did see a few cool-looking masks, a Photoshopped same face, zingy ethnic colors, and a dark indigo swath that matched an outfit. But generally, Tokyoites, usually so concerned about appearances, just gave up and gave in to hospital white. On the train, the masks formed a giant ellipsis down the row—white, white, white.

There were the eyes. I looked into them more than I ever did before. Japanese have always been great at the side glance, the peripheral taking in of everything around them.

It's an urban necessity. But the masks intensified the eyes as if the communicative power of the whole face was compressed into the eyes. Floating over the blank canvas of a white mask, everyone's eyes became more sensitive, more alive. But the eyes can't do all the work a full face can. Much was lost.

Tokyo has always been a city of secret spaces, dark interiors, and the unseen insides of offices and private homes. Frankly, few people could claim to have seen much of the inside of Tokyo at all. You can see the few spaces you can access through money, connection, or invitation, but not much else. In Tokyo, you're only invited into a small fraction of interiors. But when the front doors on all the faces were closed, it felt like the entire city was shuttered.

It broke my heart that one of the greatest joys of the city—the endless flow of faces—was blockaded. The city became a walking cloister, oddly like a Shinto Shrine, where a *sudare* bamboo screen always covers the innermost space. The Shinto gods are there but remain unseen. Tokyoites were there but half erased.

I noticed this feeling in my classroom, where we all stayed masked for those two years. Over my career, I'd learned to read students' faces for unspoken questions and hints of confusion. Reading faces lets me respond in real time to the atmosphere and flow of discussions and presentations. But when that essential tool was removed, it made me miss a beat and misread their clues.

But it also made me miss the satisfaction of seeing realization on their faces and the welcome surprise of understanding. Masks turned them into blank pages. I was forced to ask students more about what they thought, which wasn't bad, but it was slower than a quick read of their faces. I missed out on *their* feedback. I couldn't see if they were getting it, satisfied, confused, or what. I left each class with a disturbing uncertainty.

Outside my classroom, Tokyo became slower to read. The city felt far away without faces, even when I was in the middle of it. As a writer, observing people's faces and imagining their stories was my daily practice, my mental sudoku. Its absence left a flabby distance from my work and from myself. The inspiration for imagination—faces—had been stifled.

I felt cut off from the interplay with the unknown, the posing of questions, and the imaginative spur of people-watching. Without the daily flow of faces, Tokyo was converted into a reasonably safe place for a few years, but it just wasn't itself.

Hidden faces on unfilled trains

White petals hiding worlds inside.

Breaking Homes

Every few weeks, as I ride my bike to the station, I come across a home split open. The front wall is ripped away, exposing a hollowed-out interior. I see stately traditional homes chewed up by backhoes, spit into trucks, and hauled away. I stop to watch walls and posts topple, roofs collapse, and concrete foundations ripped from the earth—another home broken to pieces to haul away on a flatbed truck.

Metal bathtubs are crumpled, in-wall clocks left at their last electrified hour, a too-big chest left in its decades-long corner. The upstairs bedrooms are no longer private, the kitchens are no longer warm and welcoming, and the front hallway becomes a shambles of wood and tile. Piping and wiring dangle like branches broken in a storm. I feel like I'm witnessing a crime.

But actually, I'm witnessing Tokyo's process of renewing itself and re-dividing land. Old homes with gardens are too much trouble for young people, so they're sold off, ripped down, and the lot subdivided. The economics doesn't interest me. It's the process of tearing down the homes that I can't take my eyes off. Tokyo is usually so hidden. Walls, doors, prohibited areas, and windowless expanses are the norm. The violation of that norm always shocks me.

Wall after wall is smashed and splintered. The guts of houses I'd ridden by for years are opened to the air like in photos of wartime bombings. You can see what was long hidden—the inner stage for the dramas of bedroom and kitchen, the relaxation of tatami and bath, the secrets of closet and toilet. All are left hanging out like morning wash for any passerby to ogle. I can't help but stop and take a few photos.

It's mesmerizing to witness the interior become exterior, construction on rewind, and the walls that protected one family's world stripped away. It's hard not to peer at the violent end of something so private. The creaking and shredding of walls, staircases, balconies, and floors seem to be the home's last gasp, its death rattle.

In one Toshiro Mifune film, his good-guy samurai character takes revenge against a rice-hoarding landlord by chopping the central pillar of the storehouse with a single swing of his sword. The roof and walls collapse, and the starving peasants surge in to reclaim the rice. I laughed the first time I saw that film, not believing it. But now I know it's true.

It's not one sword cut, of course. It is a week of backhoe thrusts, a bit of yanking and tearing, and some well-aimed jackhammering. And it's over. Most Tokyo homes are made of wood. If it's an older home, it's made of weathered, termite-eaten, humidity-wetted wood. Old Japanese homes are not much more than wood and memories.

The glass windows are removed before the real action gets underway, but I'm surprised that pictures, decorations, furniture, and tatami mats are often left in place—along with toilets. There is no reuse value there. The metal bathtubs are crumpled like silver paper and saved to hold debris. Workers (roof specialists) toss the roof tiles hand to hand down to the truck like a fire bucket brigade.

Unlike in America, it is rare in Tokyo to visit other people's homes. Entertaining is done outside, at bars or restaurants. I've been into one or two of my Japanese colleagues' homes, but not many. And even then, I went to one room for entertaining, plus maybe the toilet or kitchen. It's not like the grand home tour Americans like to give visitors.

I love looking inside homes or offices from the train. Though you can gawk at various interiors the train passes, it's only for a few seconds, less on an express. I never get to indulge my observing eyes and imagination fully enough. It lets me see the parts of Tokyo I can't usually see.

It must be embarrassing for the family to think of their home exposed, their choice of colors and patterns, their layout, and their past splayed open. It embarrasses me, and it's never my home. It's the stuff of nightmares, wandering in public naked, your house exposed. Watching these teardowns is like seeing time reversed. It's obscene in a way, lacking respect for the dead. But there's no other way to do it.

I do have respect, but it's fascinating to watch the backhoe attachment eating its way through the house like a giant metal termite. In collapse, the homes appear to be nothing more than dust and sawdust held together by the magic spell "home." There is often so much dust that one worker sprays water to keep it from drifting around the neighborhood. Dust to dust.

I'm always intrigued by the skill and daring of the workers. The driver works the controls, moving forward to crunch through a section of wood, backing up to let it drop, and surging forward again. The pincher teeth can pick up a beam to wield like a club to whack down ceilings, buckle a staircase, or bust through a wall. The stackers stay out of the way by the truck, setting wood boards and beams to haul away. They work in narrow spaces, small tracts with homes on either side. Scaffolds hold protective tarps to keep pieces from flipping around.

One rainy morning, I asked the guy in charge of stacking the wood on the truck how long one home took. He told me most two-story homes took about a week. What took the most time was separating materials into insulation, metal, concrete, and wood. Old tatami mats are often slipped under the backhoe treads for traction. I asked where he recycled everything and what you'd get for all the materials. He looked confused. "It's all *gomi* (trash)," he told me. Then he got back to work.

It must be a sad job to pack a family's furniture, bathtubs, sinks, fixtures, and leftover junk onto a truck and haul it away. I wonder whether the workers can hear echoes of the conversations, laughs and cries, arguments, celebrations, dinners, baths, and exclamations of love that must have taken place inside that home.

Instead of asking, I ride off on my bike, wondering, once the last board of wood is stacked, the dirt packed down, and the public road hosed clean, if anything remains to remember the lives lived there. It couldn't all be *gomi*. But in Tokyo, it's the land that holds value, not the past lives, not the old buildings, not the materials, not even the people.

After a house is down, I keep an eye on the lot as I ride by in the following weeks, waiting for signs of the groundbreaking ceremony. Once or twice, I've chanced on the Shinto ceremony, where a priest sets up a ring of bamboo, rope, and *washi* paper with a symbolic wooden hoe, sacred *sakaki* branches, and other offerings. He intones prayers as the new owners lower their heads. The ceremony sanctifies the ground before the next home can be built.

And before the construction gets underway, the stage for

a new set of lives, what's left behind is a sprig of rice stalk set in a small mound of dirt, from which another home and another set of lives will grow in the same space once again.

Tatami Change

The three men were in and out in twenty minutes. Their only tools were a marking pen and a hand-held hook. Kneeling, they marked the position with the pen before leaning down, sinking in the hook, and hoisting my tatami mats up and out of the floor. Balancing the heavy mats between hook and hand, they moved through the house in a single motion to the entryway, where they slowed to slip on their shoes, and continued to their van where they laid the mats in a neat pile in the back.

When they'd removed the twelve mats from two six-mat rooms, one upstairs and one downstairs, I followed them outside. They were taking the mats to their workshop. I wanted to go with them and spend the afternoon watching them refurbish the mats, but it was starting to snow, and I had things to do in the house before they returned.

I watched the three tatami specialists, two generations, hop into their van after promising to return that afternoon. They'd spend the day stretching new *igusa* rush matting across the top of each mat, realigning the base, repairing the spots my computer chair had crumpled, and adding new *heri* brocade borders which I'd selected from sample boards when the youngest of the tatami specialists came to my house the week before.

It was my first time having tatami replaced. I'd moved often and tatami is always changed when moving into a new place, but I didn't want to confess to the workers that we hadn't changed these mats in fifteen years, about double their expected lifetime. They could tell. Several of the mats had sunk. The top layer had shredded beneath a footrest, crumpled under a bookshelf, and worn thin beneath an office chair. I could slip a finger between a couple of the mats. They looked askance at the well-worn mats but didn't say anything. I felt embarrassed to have not done better with tatami care.

I had plenty to do before they returned. In our first-floor tatami room, a patina of grey mold covered the wood boards that had been under the mats. The tatami specialists told me the mold was rare, but my house is made of wood, and the trees and garden in the back hold the humidity. In fact, our house is like a sponge in the summer. Most of the first-floor wood flooring had already weakened and been replaced. The tatami had stayed dry and firm. It was the wood that weakened.

Bending to the mold, I suddenly felt very un-Japanese. I loved the tatami but hadn't taken proper care of it. I realized that over the years of living in Japan, I'd not only been surrounded by Japanese culture, but also had the most Japanese of cultural objects right underfoot. I lacked attention and enough respect.

The parquet floor in the other rooms had always had pieces pop loose from time to time, another victim of humidity. But I keep good, strong glue and a weight to press them back into place. I've developed my own technique for the wood, but gluing pieces of the floor back in place could hardly compare to what the tatami artisans accomplish.

Their workshop's website said they'd done 36,000 installations. Even divided over two generations, it was an amazing number. You could see their experience in their practiced way of marking, planning, and handling the tatami. You could see the dedication in their faces when they complained that young Japanese didn't want tatami anymore. It was too much effort to clean and care for. No one wanted to roll out and roll up a futon every day. They wanted a mattress on a solid wood floor. Tatami was an endangered species.

With the tatami gone, the house felt empty and hollow. My steps echoed eerily, and with the support wood exposed, it was like staring into a dark basement, even though it was less than a few fingers deep. The rooms looked emptier than I'd ever seen them, like the house had been cracked in half. I cleaned up and waited, looking away.

The tatami specialists pulled up in front of our house in the late afternoon. I came out to greet them with the snow still coming down. They opened the back of the van and, one by one, hustled the dozen large mats back inside, sure-footed over the snow as they hauled the heavy mats out of the van and up the stairs.

The older of the three came inside to read the marks on the bottom of the mats and make sure they were going in the right place. On the bottom, they'd written notes with the secret to the puzzle. Directing the younger men to slip the mats into place, it took two of them to align the borders side by side and top to bottom. The mats fit snugly into their pre-determined place. And the house filled up with the rich, grassy aroma of tatami.

I thought they were done, but the two younger men started pulling up the mats one by one as the older master cut a slice of old tatami to slip under and level them out. He walked back and forth testing the balance in his socks, his feet as much a tool as his hands. Where it was off, he cut a slice of old tatami and slipped it below until all the mats and the *heri* borders lined up even more perfectly.

When he was finally satisfied, he invited me to step on the new mats. I took off my house slippers and stepped forward. The new green tatami gave back a nice crackle. The aroma welled up with each step. I knew that would fade, and the tatami color would gradually turn golden, the working of time itself part of the craftsmanship, but the fresh meadowy feeling of it was startling. Walking across the new tatami, the whispering crunch called out an invitation to drink a cup of tea, meditate, or do nothing. Tatami is more of a giant sofa than a floor.

As I walked back and forth over the new mats, I thought back to how much we'd used, and maybe abused, the tatami over the years. We hadn't just walked or sat or slept on them. At home parties, students had spilled sangria and beer. Friends had dropped gravy and guacamole. I'd flopped down in the summer heat with only a towel between my sweaty back and the mats. At Christmas and New Year parties, we'd danced to funky music, jumping, twirling, and grinding the poor reeds underfoot. The tatami handled it all, but it could only do so much.

The first year I lived in Japan, I saw a row of women in a Kyoto temple bend over like a football scrimmage line with cloths in hand. At a signal, they scuttled forward, bottoms in the air, rubbing the cloths across the tatami while a massive gold Buddha looked down on their efforts. They worked back and forth in a steady line, cleaning the dust from the vast expanse of the hundred-some-mat interior. Wood forms the pedestal for the Buddha, but it's tatami that covers the sacred interior of most temples, a springboard for the spiritual.

The largest tatami room in the world is the two-thousand-mat Jodo Shinshu (Pure Land) Buddhist temple in Toyama. I can't imagine cleaning, much less replacing the tatami in a room that size. Our six mats couldn't compare, but I felt the new mats brought something sacred to our house just the same. They smelled clean and soft, with a stately presence that flowed outward. The adjoining wood-floored rooms seemed like a frame around the main exhibit—the mats.

Tatami has a long history. In paintings of old Japan, the emperor always sits on tatami mats while the lower-ranking aristocrats, statesmen, and feudal lords kneel on cushions set on wood. Since the eighth century, the nation's politics were decided atop tatami. At the top of elaborate Girls' Day Doll exhibits, the emperor and empress sit on—of course—a miniature block of tatami. Tatami reached the homes of commoners only in the 17th century. Having tatami at home elevates and ennobles one's home.

Tatami is more than a floor. It's bedding, a chair, and a sofa but also expresses aesthetic and cultural values. Japanese homes are often divided into *washitsu*, Japanese rooms, and *yoshitsu*, or Western-style rooms. More and more, though, *washitsu* doesn't fit big-city lifestyles. People no longer want—or need—a multi-functional space that can alternate between living room, bedroom, dining room, and chill-out room. They want separate rooms for separate purposes without having to stoop over and dry-wipe reed mats.

In every culture, inside and outside are marked through conventions and customs, but in Japan, tatami is the inside of the inside. All Japanese visitors take their shoes off at the front door, but most also pause at the edge of a tatami room, leaving indoor sandals just outside the tatami. In that sense, the tatami artisans had restored the innermost sanctity of our house.

The three tatami-makers swept up the last few loose bits of tatami they'd cut and rechecked the mats. Their eyes worked over our redone room. They brought to bear their experience, craft, and traditional values to transform our home and the life we lead there. It wasn't just replacing a new set of tatami. It was re-establishing an entire cultural aesthetic. I followed their gaze as they made sure it was perfect and perfectly Japanese.

After satisfying themselves, the tatami craftsmen seemed to hesitate as they headed to the door. Could they trust me? They'd have to. They told me to call if there were any problems. But what problem could there be? Tatami wasn't some machine or object that could break. It was a resilient artifact based on a complex set of beliefs installed in our home to dignify our life.

After the tatami craftsmen drove off, I returned inside, walked to the tatami, wiggled my feet, enjoying the delicious crackle of the new reeds, and then dropped down and stretched out, sinking into the aroma of fresh tatami in what felt like a new home, a new attitude to life. I promised myself to take better care of it and learn its lessons.

Bone *Sake*

I've dealt with plenty of fish bones during my time in Tokyo, but nothing like bone sake—a sheet of bones deep-fried until they become crisp as potato chips and just as chompable, dropped into a big glass of sake. I don't enjoy fish bones like some people do, and I tend to order boneless pieces when I have the choice. But on occasion, I don't mind chewing fish meat with bones inside if the taste is good enough to overcome the boniness, that is, if there's texture, taste, or another pleasure involved. Pure bones are another thing.

The drink I ordered at a cozy, old-style *izakaya* in Ogikubo, the boniness seemed to be the entire goal, as if all the other fish flavors had been stripped away and what was left was the pure, direct taste of bone. After decades of eating and drinking anything set before me, I wondered if I had at last hit some cultural wall?

Japanese food is varied and complex, so I often order things out of curiosity after seeing them cross the restaurant in the hands of the wait staff. "What's that?" I'll whisper when they come to my table, or I'll search the menu for the never-seen-before dish and just order it. But this time, half-joking and half-adventurous, I looked at the hand-written sign for "bone *sake*" hanging on the wall—two simple characters: bone and alcohol—and thought: What could go wrong? My wife rolled her eyes in wifely censure, but I insisted.

The waiter nodded approvingly when I ordered it, normally a sign that I'm in for something unique, something that "only Japanese would order." I knew that to be the case with the bone *sake* when the waiter set the glass down on the table. It was clearly bones in *sake*, not some poetic, metaphoric name alluding to something different. It was a complete fish skeleton soaking in a glass of clear alcohol, like a preserved specimen from some dusty nineteenth century laboratory.

The waiter pulled off the wood top, flicked a lighter and set it aflame. The small booth filled with the smell of bones and burning alcohol. Then, he quickly set the wood top back on and left me and my wife alone with the bones floating in the clear alcohol.

The flame seemed to have crisped the top part of the bone and cartilage. A few hard, white bits floated to the surface as I swirled the warm glass. The aroma cut through all the other delicious smells of the place—raw fish, grilled meat, tempura, fried vegetables and fresh *sake*. All I could smell was scorched bone.

The taste was weakly *sake* and strongly fish bone, stronger than any bone I had ever tasted before. On top, the flavor was charcoal-ish, an organic burn. Below, the bone flavor came out fully. I had to breathe to take a second sip. Bone.

After that, I sipped hesitantly, wondering if the bone flavor would strengthen as it soaked. For the first time in a very long time, I felt I simply could not finish something. The very words were unappetizing, the syllables hard as bones.

I leaned back on the cushions in the comfy wood booth and peered around the *izakaya* to see if anyone else had ordered the same. The other customers were all enjoying nice, cold glasses of *sake*, iced *shochu* and big mugs of beer.

In front of me floated a fish skull, jaw, fins, ribs, spine, vertebrae, and tail.

Japanese food often seems to push the drinker and diner into a clear, direct encounter with nature's bounty. Raw fish is that exactly—the real taste of fish without any cultural interference, the same taste you'd have if stranded on a boat in the ocean and forced to fish for yourself. Other preparation methods, the fermentation of *shiokara* (squid guts) or *natto* (soybeans), are cultural techniques that enhance and ripen the food to bring your taste buds closer to the pure, original taste.

I sat there not drinking, deciding what to order instead. My wife had already declined a taste repeatedly, scowling at me each time I offered. I increasingly felt like I should be—or maybe already was—dissecting the bones, studying them, and sketching them like a zoologist or Renaissance-era medical student.

I tried to sip a bit more, but it wasn't like drinking exactly. The entire effect was something else altogether—a bone-to-bone connection as if being punched or struck by a hard object.

The bone *sake* brought me closer to the essence of bone, a place I wasn't sure I wanted to be. When you get to the bones, how much closer can you get to anything else? There's nothing inside fish bones, no marrow, no blood cell production; it's just bone.

The drink seemed to be sending me back to that moment when fish leapt up onto land, bringing their bones out of the salty water into the air. And back into myself. We are, after all, like fish bones at some point when we develop through the stages of evolution as fetuses in the womb. Was that the point, I wondered? But of course, there was no one to ask.

I felt a little disappointed with myself. I had always been proud of being open enough to eat every animal, insect, vegetable, fruit, or concoction set in front of me over the years, but I had to admit defeat. The fish bones, so small, so frail and usually disposable, were more powerful than I was. My curiosity, half-joking, half-macho, had met its match. I had to concede.

A couple of beers, some familiar *yakitori and* comforting *tofu* set me back into a lighter mood, but I would think about my defeat for several days after until the taste, the feel, the boniness finally disappeared from where it had settled inside my body, where I had started to worry it would remain forever. It possibly always will.

Tokyo Arrows

A long hallway at Heathrow Airport once totally freaked me out. Jetlagged after flying in from Tokyo, I followed the one sign directing me towards baggage check. After a few minutes, another hallway cut to the left. No advertising, no sign, just a hallway. Other jetlagged people stumbled forward, but immobilized, I turned back with my mind in a muddle. I realized what I needed was an arrow.

Living in Tokyo, I've become addicted to arrows. Over the years of commuting, I've grown dependent on arrows to guide, direct, protect, and keep me moving in the right direction. In Tokyo, arrows stream pedestrians. There is no shortage of either, all the time, everywhere.

How many total arrows are plastered over Tokyo station walls, signs, street corners, and sidewalks? As many as there are directions, as many as there are people to follow them. The arrows rise constantly over the heads of pedestrians like thought bubbles of where to go.

You can tell how crowded an area can get by how many arrows there are. In stations like Shibuya and Shinjuku, arrows abound, flying overhead like the first attack in an old Japanese samurai movie. In some neighborhoods, the arrows are confined to discrete signs pointing the way to a clinic or local museum. But they are always there.

Fortunately! Without those arrows, Tokyo could not function. What would happen, I sometimes wonder, if all the arrows were removed? Everyone in Tokyo would head the wrong way—or worse—half of Tokyo would head the wrong way. The city would grind to a confused, irritated halt, like me in Heathrow.

Arrowless chaos would not be pretty. People would be searching overhead for guidance, stopping suddenly, backtracking, finger-searching cellphone maps, bumping into each other, barely missing bumping into each other—committing all the disruptions that never happen in a typical, arrow-laden Tokyo day.

No one looks good lost. Being lost in Tokyo is one of the few times stone-faced Tokyoites openly express exasperation and embarrassment. Their faces scrunch up, frown, redden, and squint. It's unpleasant to see. Though Tokyoites generally hurry past the lost and confused, the internal thought of stopping to help always pops up, slowing even the confidently directed.

I don't like to be embarrassed should other people think I don't know where I'm going. The arrows let me slip smoothly into Tokyo's pedestrian traffic and appear to know my way around better than I do. When going someplace new, I can glance arrow-ward and find where I'm headed. I'm spared the shame of misdirection.

Most times, though, following arrows is less of a choice than a necessity. In peak crowds, to go against the arrows is to invite disaster. A crowd moving in the right direction can speed you along, but a crowd with even one person trying to buck the flow throws the entire crowd out of whack. To change direction, you have to flow downstream, angling gently to the side until you can find a saving pillar, wall corner, or other opening to reverse course. Then, you look for the arrows back the other way.

Arrows proliferate when construction is going on, which is often. You can sense the irritation when temporary arrows prod people out of their ingrained routes. The short-term arrows are pasted on walls and pillars, apologetic for the inconvenience.

Over the years, I've resigned myself to trusting the arrows. Following one wrongly read arrow can put you a long way from where you want to be. Ignoring the arrows can spill you out of the wrong station exit with a twenty-minute walk to right yourself. Of course, you need to follow the arrows back through the maze, sighting more carefully and paying closer attention.

Though I appreciate the smooth flow and admit the simple, obvious utility of the arrows, I sometimes feel like I'm being ordered around, as if I'm filling in some pre-written pattern. I feel like I've been trained, like a Pavlovian dog, for the trick of walking in a crowd. I'm crowd-trained, and generally, I perform obediently.

Some days, I feel like I'm led from arrow to arrow as if playing a board game. I feel like I'm moving towards the prize at the end, rewarded by not smashing into people. On other days, the arrows feel like commands: relentless, inescapable, unavoidable. *Keep marching!* I like the arrows ordering other people around, just not ordering me around. But I always capitulate.

And there are more and more arrows all the time. It's strange that the more cellphone navigation apps there are, the more arrows are put up. Are we more in need of being herded than ever? Is the proliferation because of the foreign tourist boom? Are people just more lost than ever?

I wonder if there's some other symbolism underneath it all. The phallic shape, even when bent and curved, is undeniable. Little triangle-rectangle shapes move the entire population of the city around. Could it be that easy? Are they symbols of power? Some kind of mind-body control? A message from the deep state? Or are the arrows a step forward in urban planning and civility? A thoughtful, helpful politeness in a refined city?

All of those, I guess. The arrows keep everyone on track, not just physically, but also psychologically. They are visual shouts of *ganbatte,* don't give up, persevere. They float overhead, encouraging and hopeful, a reassuring sign that there *IS* a direction, and you are heading in it, while your passage, marked by each arrow, one after the next, is left behind.

Tokyo Toads

When spring comes to Tokyo, most people look up. The *ume* plum blossoms and *anzu* apricot trees are the opening act for the main attraction of *sakura* cherry blossoms. The entire city, for once, looks in the same direction. Everyone rolls their head back like a newborn bird and receives the sustenance of cherry blossom beauty from above. I do, too.

But for the past few years, I've also started to look down. The mud, grass, and rainwater draw my eyes to the earth. What I relish finding there, at spring blossom time, are toads. Rather amazingly for a city of this size, speed and pavement, my back garden has toads—two last year, five this year, and hundreds of tadpoles. Their arrival is just as sure a sign of spring as the *sakura*, and just as impressive.

Yet, most people cringe at the word "toad" and hum delightedly at "cherry blossoms." That's why March and April's weather reports end with the cherry blossom schedules from Okinawa to Hokkaido but never report on toad mating season. That hardly seems fair. *Hanami* flower-viewing, yes, but why not *ushigaeru-mi* toad-viewing too?

I love when the toads first emerge from their winter hibernation. Frumpy and ponderous, they don't jump, they crawl, and not very gracefully, as if still half-asleep, as if their limbs were made for something else. They are baggy-skinned blobs, creatures of gravity, in balance with its pull. Toads dig down, relishing the earth, burrowing face-first into the mud and muck humans avoid.

Blossoms are the opposite of that, resisting the earth and refusing gravity. The blossoms are light enough to catch the breeze and dance and dart like baby kites. They carry your feeling skyward, billowing with life. Framed against a blue, even a grey, sky, they tickle your eyeballs with their flight and final fall to earth.

Toads seem half-dead most of the time, patiently waiting for the next insect or once-a-year chance to mate. They stay in place, prodded to move only by predators or procreation. They seem content where they are, half-hidden under some clump of forest grass or wedged under a rock. They amble and stall, their directions and desires pre-decided.

Cherry blossoms redecorate the outdoors with a brushstroked ceiling and red, white, and pink carpeting. Lit up by the sun, they layer outdoor spaces—gardens, waterways, sidewalks—with desire. If there were cherry blossoms all year round, maybe no one would pay them much attention, but they come and go so quickly that it's impossible not to feel their power, to say how beautiful they are before they're gone.

Toads don't draw attention at all. They blend in with colors that you see all year round. Toad skin is like tree bark, mottled and rough. With black dots, greenish splashes, dark browns, and dull beige patches on the chest, I often don't see them until it's nearly too late. Unlike the showy, brilliant blossoms, toads exhibit barely a shift from winter colors.

But when I stumble over one lurking in the dark parts of the garden, I always feel surprised and laugh. Toads are nature's silent comedians, the straight-faced act that delivers simple amusement. They seem so improbable a creature to carry on in a city like Tokyo, even in the thin slice of nature in our backyard.

When it rains, they bounce up and down in my little

pond, clucking and barking, dunking below the surface, resting two eyes just above, drinking water through their skin. They sometimes tumble off the little stairway of rocks I made for them to get in and out of the pond, a slapstick pratfall, like some half-broken toy. They land on the grass and roll over, and I laugh on cue.

It's a given that cherry blossoms are the billowy stage curtains around the brevity of life, a frame for grasping the fleeting beauty of the world. But laughing is a kind of beauty too, and another way of apprehending the world. I always enjoy a toad laugh, especially since nature doesn't joke too often.

And then they mate. The female carries the male around on her back, and together, they slather long strings of fertilized egg casings back and forth through the pond. It takes several days, and the male rides her the whole time. After the eggs are strung, the male and female go their separate ways, both eyeing me for a moment before they creep back to snooze until summer's insect-eating season.

The hundreds of tadpoles they produce have a greater claim to beauty. The little black swimmers slip out of their sacs and start wriggling immediately, speeding up under the sun and slowing down with the evening's cold. One by one, they become tight, black mini-toads, cute and comic, moving jerkily until plucked off by some passing bird or, beating the odds, surviving who knows where.

And though only a fraction of the tadpoles survive, their short lives don't stir the same poetic feeling as cherry blossoms. When the blossoms fall, it's an emotional fall. We want to see them keep going, to fly away, though they never do. The feeling of dirt, moss, muck, and water plants does not inspire the same sense of transcendence. It's more about rootedness.

Toads don't stir lofty aspirations. They are horizontal creatures, practical, bound to forward routes, and never out in the sun for long. They emerge from hibernation and pursue reproduction. They are at ease with the earth's surface, moving as if mapping it, at times hardly distinguishable from the mud they tunnel into. But like the blossoms, they always return on schedule.

And just as cherry trees have their own history going back to the Heian Period and expanding through the Tokugawa Era, toads too, have a history, though it's less often told. The Musashino plains of western Tokyo, where I live, were long the hunting fields for the samurai of old Edo. The area was a place to race horses, practice falconry, run large dogs, and bag edible creatures. I'm not sure what toads did then, but they must have been somewhere in the ecosystem. That hunting culture is gone, but the toads remain.

Toads, I read, are not nomadic, staying close to their origins, often reproducing in the same waters where they were spawned. They do not adapt well if transported to another place, and toad websites advise against this. Cherry trees, however, can be replanted almost anywhere. And in Tokyo, they are. But toads are tied to the earth where they were born, surviving on their ancestors' turf. I'm startled to think the toads in my backyard must have an ancient lineage.

When we first moved to our house, one toad used to join us on summer nights. It surprised me every time and drew a chuckle. I'd think getting into our backyard is not so easy for a toad. It's lined with a cinderblock wall. But toads have their ways. He or she (she, I think) would waddle through the tall grass at night to sit right on the step at the edge of our porch. While we finished our dinner and sipped wine, the toad slurped insects drawn by our solar lights.

I always toasted that toad with a generous, drunken welcome for joining us in our backyard. But I suppose it was really the toad who was welcoming us to her family's territory.

Now, after many years of spring toads, they seem as much a part of early spring as cherry blossoms, and for me, just as anticipated. Of course, I still love cherry blossoms. Who doesn't?

But as the years add up, I feel the need to look down at the earth as well as up to the branches and sky above. A good laugh with the garden toads always complements—and enhances—the feelings from the cherry blossoms at the start of another spring.

Ramen Everywhere

A few weeks ago, I met a former student who is now a salesman. He travels all over Tokyo to meet clients. I asked him how he survived such a tiring job running all over the city every day. He admitted it was tough, but he said his job was made easy, in fact, a pleasure, because of one thing—the Ramen Database.

I also love ramen and use that site. So, when my student told me he used the site almost daily, I felt like I had found a brother. I also felt jealous he gets to eat more ramen than I do. The outstanding achievement of the Ramen Database is to map the entire country—for ramen! Every noodle shop in the whole country is on there. It achieves the Japanese sense of completion and perfection. It's an echo chamber of the best sort, ensuring you won't want to eat anything but ramen after reading it.

We both appreciated how fantastic it is to know the entirety of Japan is mapped out for one of our favorite experiences. You can go anywhere in the country without worrying you will end up ramen-less. Ramen is like a cult. People can be fanatics. The website is its most sacred site, like mapping every temple or national treasure of Japan.

Ramen stirs passions. Ramen lovers have opinions on everything from the noodles' curl to the bean sprouts' freshness to the chefs' technique of shaking off the water. And it is not like comparing ramen is easy. You can't line them up and try one after the next. Few people can eat more than one bowl a day. But people do remember their reactions in tremendous detail, write them down, and upload them to the Ramen Database.

Ramen and technology seem an unlikely pairing since the cold, hard feel of a computer or cellphone seems far removed from the steamy warmth of a bowl of noodles. But what better use of technology? I love being in a strange part of the city or the country and being able to thumb my cellphone thinking, "Deliver me to a great bowl of noodles," and it happens!

Even though Japan is perhaps the most obsessively mapped country in the world, the ramen database feels as much practical necessity as obsession. Japanese cities are hard to navigate, so before the database, some of the best ramen places could only be found by accident or word of mouth. You had to walk by a place a few times, have someone tell you, or try your luck. Thanks to the site, the best ramen shops are now much easier to find, the country is more transparent, and a lot less hungry.

Ramen is also rising to the heights of Michelin stars and international culinary guidebooks, with at least one Hong Kong-style ramen shop in the stylish Omotesando Hills complex being awarded a Michelin star. Still, ramen remains one of the most beloved of Japanese foods. A glance inside any ramen shop at lunchtime will show you that ramen is taken very seriously, not just on the internet but in real life too. The places are packed.

And should you be stuck at home, or stuck in a viral pandemic, you can just order frozen ramen, thanks to the online service Takumen, a play on the words for delivery and ramen. I'm addicted to ramen, so the pandemic put me into withdrawal. The holy triumvirate of home food delivery—pizza, soba, and sushi—wasn't enough. Even the recent food delivery services bringing everything from *tonkatsu* deep-fried pork cutlets to spicy Mexican tacos rarely included high-end ramen.

Fortunately, though, Tokyo's intensive consumer culture leaves no point of sale unrealized. Delivery of frozen ramen—from some of the best ramen masters in Japan—is maybe the only good thing to come out of the pandemic. New master chef sites offer ramen from the highest-ranked shops in Japan sent to your door.

The ramen delivery sites prepare packets of broth, noodles, and fixings, freeze them, and deliver them frozen. I nestle them into the freezer. The weight of the packets is the first clue that this is not the light fare of store-bought instant ramen. It's the weight of Japan's food culture entering your home. *Irrashaimase*!

On home ramen day, I open the freezer and select a flavor from Fukuoka or Sapporo or some other ramen-crazed part of the country. I boil the soup bag for ten minutes and heat the noodles in three. My wife likes to add green leafy vegetables, a boiled egg, or nori, and we put out pickled vegetables for balance. But what I'm waiting for is that first sip of the broth and the mouthfeel of the noodles between my teeth. At my own table!

Though in a hurry, I took time to read the instructions. They explain the background, give tips on heating, and suggest additions without divulging the inner art every ramen chef keeps secret. The instructions reveal their worry that the noodles will not be prepared to their specifications. Some chefs don't trust an amateur home chef with the temperature, timing, and mixing, but thankfully, some do and take the time to explain. Their pride in every drop of broth is the traditional Japanese attention to artisanal creativity and craft.

I'll admit there's a laziness and love of convenience on my part. I don't have to get on a train to scurry all over the city, don't have to wait in line, and don't have to mess with sitting at a narrow counter. At home, I can flop onto my sofa for a post-lunch snooze, something you can't do in ramen places.

But convenience is not the point—just the opposite. Ordered-in frozen ramen recreates the excitement of going to an actual shop. It commandeers the kitchen. Pots, bowls, strainers, and long cooking chopsticks must be lined up and readied. As I run through the steps, the house fills with a deliciously sour, soupy aroma.

And then, the meal begins. And then, the bowl takes over. I bow like a penitent, intone "*Itadakimasu*," and partake.

And yet, as great as this all is, and as necessary during the pandemic, ordering this frozen DIY project makes me wonder if I'm missing something, even while I'm getting something.

Over my years of ramen excursions, I've enjoyed going to new parts of the city, checking out the people in line, elbowing into a counter, and soaking in the powerful aromas of broth simmering since dawn. I miss the condiments that line the table, the TV turned to some silly program, and even scooting aside to let someone come in or go out in the cramped space.

I especially miss the ballet of ramen creation. It's no fun watching yourself make ramen in your own kitchen, but it's always a magical performance to watch even the most overworked ramen chef behind any counter. It's the difference between having a Buddha statue on your bookshelf and kneeling in front of a massive gold Buddha in a thousand-year-old temple. The chefs perform the rituals and rites of ramen with practiced ease.

The freshness, saltiness, balance of oils and broths, and mouthfeel are all the same. But maybe it's not just the taste that matters. Ramen doesn't engage only one sense; it engages all five. Or six, if you believe that kind of thing. (With ramen, I do.) Convenient as it is, home ramen diminishes the ramen experience.

However, home frozen ramen delivery does conquer distance. Chefs and ramen aficionados all over Japan take special pride in local flavors and variations, so I'm delighted to taste ramen from places I'm not likely to go in some time. Still, I'd rather go in person. I want the story that goes with the in-person experience. Ramen always turns into a story.

But if you can have it at home, what's the experience? Is it only the taste? What happens to the ambiance of the place? The excitement of waiting in line? The boxes of ingredients in the corner? If ramen is just the packet and the noodles, and can be made by oneself, does that move it into the mass consumer system that the best ramen places, by their very existence, refute?

There is something about great art, craft, and culture that resists packaging, shipping, and reproduction. Ramen is not just a product with a story—it's a philosophy of resistance to the factory-made "food" production system. It is rooted in culture and thrives on sensory experience. Can that be imported whole?

The question itself is absurd. You might as well consider ordering *butoh* dancers or arranging a *mikoshi* festival parade through your living room. And yet, frozen ramen is an outstanding lunch once it's heated, arranged, and set in a bowl on my dining room table.

I miss a vibrant chef, a harried sous-chef, the ramen-lovers in a row. No one says much in ramen places, but their body language does. Salarymen, single women, workers, and students unwind when their bowls arrive on the counter in front of them. Their shoulders loosen as they snap open chopsticks and pick up a spoon. The chef observes his audience, reading reactions like a musician on stage. It's a shop-wide, silent conversation that no home ramen can match.

Maybe that's what art and culture do in public. They provide not just comfort but a reminder that you need culture because other people need it too. That's a large part of what I missed during the pandemic—the quietly shared experience of cultural delight, the feeling that what I love is also loved by others. Tokyoites enjoy their public culture best when it's enjoyed together.

I prefer to eat my ramen in the original shop, but there are only so many lunches in life. So, I set aside my perfectionistic authentic tendencies from time to time and eat the frozen ones at home. Life's just too short not to compromise now and again.

Part Four
Teaching in Tokyo

Introduction

Teaching is my day job and takes up most of my time. But it also puts me in contact with students and indirectly with their families, and it puts me with colleagues, working, arguing, and figuring things out. My students affect me in more ways than I can squeeze into these essays about teaching. In some sense, they're my primary contact with Japanese society and culture.

My workplace is the source of most of my aggravation living in Japan. I've rarely had huge conflicts outside of work. However, university work is divided into two realms: dealing with students and suffering with duties, meetings, and obligations. I'm only writing about the student side here. It's by far the more interesting side. The work side deserves a separate book, maybe after I retire.

I don't often have conflicts with students—the conflicts are all theirs—but I help them with their conflicts. I interact with them, but like any educator, I often want education to be my way. But that rarely happens. The factors that form the pressures of students' lives are ones that I can offer advice about but cannot shield them from. It's a cliché, but I do learn as much from them as they do from me.

People always ask me what language I use in my university work. Working with students is all in English. Everything else is almost all Japanese. My department is an English department, so the office staff are fluent in English, but outside of that, meetings, forms, offices, and information are all in Japanese.

For me, working with students is my main window

opening into Japan. The jazz world and close friends provide other windows, but I rarely see the turmoil and uncertainty of everyday life through them. I don't see the hopes and aspirations as much, either. Friends and jazz musicians are set. Students are very much works in progress, but because of that, I can observe how individuals grow and develop. University forms them, and that process is, in many ways, part of the deep culture.

William Carlos Williams wrote a wonderful essay in which he said he couldn't be a poet without being a doctor and couldn't work as a doctor without writing poetry. As aggravating as some school days are with pointless meetings, endless email, picky rules, and pressure to be an accountant, secretary, and form-filler, I've come to appreciate Williams' insight about work and writing and find that it's truer with each passing year.

Turnabout is Fair Play
—Wedding Speeches

"No! I am not Prince Hamlet, nor was meant to be;
   Am an attendant lord, one that will do.
   To swell a progress, start a scene or two." T. S. Eliot

In my all-English literature classes, my students are tasked with adapting to another language, handling challenging materials, working with a different teaching style, and navigating a range of cultural assumptions. Rarely have they returned the "favor" of that experience. But there is one way—by asking me to give a speech at their wedding.

My first wedding speech was for a student who had graduated seven or eight years before. When she asked me, I said sure, thinking it would be easy. But she wanted it in Japanese. "Oh, OK, no problem," I stammered, locked in by pride. I'd given speeches on Japan's public TV station, NHK, in Japanese, at the university's open campus, and in faculty meetings. How hard could it be?

Very hard, I soon realized. What did I know about how speeches were given? I was sure that any Japanese wedding speech would be expected to follow a specific form without deviation. But what was that form?

I searched frantically on the internet and found multiple examples of wedding speeches. Others had panicked before me. I surveyed the templates, unsure how to do things right. The speech types ranged from best friends to work bosses to my category, *onshi*, former teacher. I copied the phrases, looked up the kanji, and got to work. Are wedding speeches in my work contract? I don't even have a work contract. Anyway, it wasn't work exactly.

And it wasn't like any speech I'd ever given before. Japanese wedding speeches involve a perfect storm of formal language, ingrained expectations, and carefully scripted performance. There was little room to improvise and a lot of room to fill up. I didn't see any way outside the strictures. Was my growing panic the same thing my students felt before their presentations?

The how-to websites also included a long list of taboos, cranking my anxiety up further. Wedding speeches must avoid words related to knives, cutting, death, or breaking things. I edited out any bad luck words that could jinx the whole marriage. It wasn't easy fitting my jokey American looseness under the unsmiling weight of Japanese formalities.

Friends fixed my grammar and corrected my pronunciation. I memorized it as best I could and practiced in my head, deleting some phrases I couldn't get my tongue around. I recorded myself, listened, and tried again. "Try to give your speech comfortably, freely, naturally, without reading directly," I tell my students. Or used to.

On the wedding day, I tucked the final copy of the speech in my jacket and headed to the wedding hall. I fidgeted on the train, practicing in my head, feeling pinched and awkward in my white wedding tie, stiff shoes, and black jacket. In class, I usually dress more casually than most of my students. Was formality always about discomfort? Did I think that while living in Japan, I could escape either one?

I also fidgeted with the thick envelope for the *goshugi*, the obligatory gift of nice, clean cash. I secured pristine, unused ten-thousand-yen bills from the service counter of a department store. Three bills would have seemed cheap, and four would mimic the sound of the Japanese word for death, another taboo. I slipped in five. I'd bought cars for less as a graduate student. I suppose it was a small refund on tuition. It turns out it was tuition for a lesson of my own.

As I sat in my assigned seat at the front of the hall, the slick master of ceremonies, an attractive woman still dreaming of being an actress, came over to confirm I would be ready. She promised to call my name loud and clear when it was time for me to ascend the podium. I wanted to run through my speech again, but didn't want to appear desperate, so I waited inside my sensei mask of false confidence.

All around me, people chatted in polite, hushed tones, introduced themselves in formal language, and sat in their assigned seats staring at the shiny plates, cutlery, and table decorations until the bride and groom entered and the spotlights followed them to the seat of honor. Engulfed in such formality, such ceremony, there are only two choices—perform well or be shamed.

There's nothing like a spotlight hitting you in a large hall to make your memory malfunction. I'd never given a speech to such a well-dressed crowd. Everyone sat in silent, rapt attention. "Be sure to prepare and practice enough," I tell my students. I wished I had, but I didn't want to embarrass my student, so I got right into it.

In the speech, I recounted a couple of anecdotes about my student, read a sonnet from Shakespeare that she'd printed out in translation for each table, and at the end, adlibbed a few comments in English, the language I use with students in class and out. I remembered most of the speech.

I think everyone applauded, but my ears were ringing as I bowed and sat down. My students don't have the luxury of a drink after giving their speeches in class, but I didn't restrain myself. Wait staff rushed over with a bottle in their white-gloved hands, and I downed a glass of champagne. Then another. I would never assign speeches in class again.

I wondered if my student, from her perch at the front surrounded by flowers, would award me points for effort or mark me down for my bumbled phrases, simplistic content, and panicky posture. And what did the room full of family and friends think? I gave my speech a B minus.

Sitting there drinking, recovering, and wondering why I hadn't studied Japanese harder, I watched as the groom's boss, a section chief at his company, got up to give his speech. He was nervous too. I wasn't the only one. But then, he pulled out several pages from his inside pocket, straightened his white tie, and started to read *his* speech!

I had spent weeks in bilingual despair, memorizing tricky syllables, mastering new phrases, and feeling my way through the fog of another language. And this native Japanese speaker was just going to read his speech? I would never try to memorize a speech again! And I never have.

But more importantly, once I quit fretting about my fumbling, I realized a lot more was going on at those weddings than following scripts, avoiding humiliation, and slurping champagne.

Template or not, wedding speeches are a testament, a confirmation, a guarantee. It's a recommendation letter delivered standing up in a big hall. I stood up for my student on one of the most important days of her life. That was an honor I never expected to get from teaching. Or maybe I wasn't a teacher there. Weddings are set deeply into the culture, wherever they occur, and might be one of its most exemplary expressions. Very much like education.

By inviting me to their wedding, my students were bringing that cultural immersion full circle. They probably imagined that since I expected that of them, it would be easy for me to do the same. It wasn't. To be a non-Japanese giving a Japanese wedding speech is to be pulled far out of one's comfort zone.

And that's precisely the experience I want for my students. Discomfort is part of learning. I drop them into poetry, short stories, films, music, and novels—complex, culture-laden stories—and ask them to handle it all in English. Compared to that, a fifteen-minute wedding speech isn't much.

Each speech has become more manageable, and I get to see more wedding activities. After the speeches, a Japanese wedding involves a lot of eating, drinking, talking, and taking photos. Those universals ease the pressure, though it's still cultural immersion. I'm always seated next to one of the bride's classmates who speaks English, a language lifeboat to keep me from drowning, but it's still intensely Japanese.

Like university courses, wedding parties move from one pre-planned minute to the next. Food arrives in steady courses like classroom assignments. The groom's parents introduce themselves, pour me a drink, and thank me for the speech. The bride's parents circulate over to meet me. There's the cake cut. There's no dancing, but everyone waltzes over to take photos with the bride and groom in choreographed huddles—childhood friends, college friends, work colleagues, and family members. We're all there.

The lights click off to show a video made from snapshots of the bride and groom from their birth through their schooling to their first date, more serious dates, and finally, the proposal and the wedding day itself. On-screen, it appears to be a straight-line progression from birth to marriage to the future. I'm there as a passing photo, a tiny sliver of their timeline, but just the same, I'm pleased to be in the story of their lives.

But after the video, when the spotlight returns to the newlyweds, my students really show me up. The most important speech of the day is the bride's final speech. Standing next to her new spouse by the doors of the wedding hall, she delivers a final farewell speech to her parents. It's always a tear-jerker.

Often, the groom has to help hold the mic—or hold the bride—because she's crying too much to stand and read. She reads her carefully prepared speech, almost a letter, delivered as if she's already far away. And it's always a far better speech than I have ever given or ever will give.

Let's be honest. Teachers fake it a lot of the time. Sure, I deliver speeches, explanations, comments, lectures, encouragement, and feedback as part of my job. Academia is filled with words, it runs on them, but the words rarely arise from the interior of my being. Has the grind of teaching depleted my words of force? How do I replenish them?

By listening to my students. Their speeches are so full of emotion that it overflows into tears, flushed skin, and shaking inside their wedding dress. The bride's farewell speech is an advanced lesson in channeling thoughts and feelings from deep inside. It's a hope-filled lesson in expressing gratitude and joy and celebrating life and commitment. Do my words do that in class?

I'm always impressed that my former students, often so awkward in English, are so fluent in the language of emotion. Standing at the door of the wedding hall, those just-married young women express something profound about their existence on the planet. What grade could I possibly give that kind of speech? It's ungradable. Fortunately, I'm not there to grade. I'm there to participate, celebrate, and learn.

I always feel honored to be invited into the nexus of their stories, especially on the day when all the stories in their life come together. In the part of my story that I call "class," I invite students into a world of written and filmed stories, and like a return gift, so important in Japanese culture, they ask me into theirs. Only theirs are real.

I'm pleased to be there as a person too, not just an *onshi*, a former teacher. It's like taking a bow at the end of a play, moving out of character and back into oneself. I play a teacher usually, but I like to return to myself at the end of the act. Of course, the champagne helps.

Giving a speech at my students' weddings, my students give me something of theirs—they share their world with me. That is something extraordinary to take home in addition to the *hikidemono* return wedding gift of tableware, regional specialties, or household goods handed out in a lavish bag at the end of the ceremony. As always, the best presents are not material ones.

It's a hard-earned gift, one I have to pay for with the sweat of my speechmaking. My students set me a challenging task, having learned, maybe partly from me, that that's the only way to learn.

Outside the Classroom

In April of every academic year, when classes are just getting into gear, I meet my students in the evening at one of the nearest stations. Everyone stands awkwardly, huddling in small groups, chatting nervously, checking cellphones, and wondering about the night ahead. We wait for stragglers or apology messages and finally head into the nightlife streets of Tokyo. For the next two hours at an *izakaya,* a Japanese-style pub, we'll eat and drink and talk together.

Many teachers around the world would never consider socializing, much less drinking with their students, but I go willingly. It's a ritual I find relevant and meaningful. Much of what I know about teaching, the university, and life in Japan has been revealed to me at such *nomikai* drinking parties.

Weeks ahead, students start organizing the *nomikai.* They select the most affordable *izakaya,* where prices are so low, I wonder how the places make a profit. We follow the leader inside the large interior and pack in tight along big tables. When the wait staff arrives, we're given the go-ahead to start our two-hour set-menu, all-you-can-drink course.

The first drinks arrive, and students push me to give a toast. I start with a heartfelt speech telling them how impressed I am with their work. The students in my seminar have chosen to do their last two years of university study by reading novels, watching films, giving presentations, and engaging in discussions—all in English.

It's hard for them to set aside the easy excuses and hard confusions of youth and stay on task.

But it's also good to get off task sometimes. I shout, "*Kanpai!*" Everyone clinks glasses, and we're off—the ritual's underway.

Students are always nervous at first. They slug down their first drink and flip through the menu, a laminated sheet or tablet ordering system. The food is often pre-set and follows a predictable series of typical dishes. We order more, talking over what looks good. They frequently try to take care of me by translating and explaining, even though I've been going to *izakaya* longer than they've been alive.

But food's an easy topic to get started with. In asking me what I do or do not like to eat and drink, they realize I'm not just their teacher, but a foreigner living in Tokyo, far from his childhood home. And I know they're out for one of the first drinking parties after reaching the legal age of twenty.

While they order, I look around at the other tables filled with salaried employees and working people who frequent this kind of cheaper *izakaya* with grungy toilets, oily floors, and weary service. Everyone's saving a buck while *nomu-*nicating (drinking-communication). Far from the tensely regimented spaces of the classroom or company office, the down-to-earth basement space allows the volume of talk to rise.

As the first dishes arrive, talk gets louder, and shyness retreats. The wait staff, usually other students in T-shirt uniforms, hustle the food out on overloaded trays clutching drink mugs like it's Oktoberfest. Students tend to choose mixed drinks that are so sweet that it pains me to taste them. I stick with beer, red wine if it's on the menu, or Japanese sake if it looks palatable.

Topics circle around safe issues at first. I love hearing about their families, and as they open up, the myth of Japanese conformity doesn't last long. Some students have lived abroad or have one parent who is not Japanese. Some dropped out of high school. They like to share who they are and what they've experienced. I ask if their parents speak English and what they do for a living so I know what stakes they've set for themselves by going all-in on English.

After we rotate seats a few times, they lean closer to open up about the mother who passed away, the autistic sibling, the father who's a rice farmer or a Buddhist priest, the alcoholic mother who dragged them to English lessons, the sister who's a nail artist and hates studying. I always ask to see their high school photos. They trot them out and eye their former selves. And then ask to see photos of me as a student. I oblige. Sharing photos is more secrets revealed.

Students often apologize in a hushed voice for a late assignment or a missed couple of classes. The reason is rarely that serious: a passing illness, a demanding boss, or a demanding school circle activity of sports, music, drama, or a speech contest. I avoid scolding them, having no reason to, and mention things like time management, how to set aside anxiety, and the importance of sleep. What would have been a lesson in obedience if it had taken place inside the university becomes a life lesson instead.

I see them searching for self-understanding. One's own behavior is often a mystery, especially when overwhelmed by depression, anxiety, or confusion. I'm always surprised at how easy they are to read and how much I like them. They are engaging in a way that's hard to identify. Maybe it's their energy, which seems boundless, even if misdirected at times. I'm surprised at how much they try to get along with me and each other.

Eventually, someone breaks the wall about boyfriends and girlfriends. A student will lean over to me and point at a friend. "She has had the same boyfriend since high school." Then, confessions spill out about a lover from another class, from a part-time job, or from the same gender. I always ask them to see a photo of their significant others. "Do you tell your parents…?" The answer is usually "No," but their romantic lives are less hidden than in the past. At the end of the night, at the station, some of them whisper to me they are not going home, but to their lovers' apartment. I raise my eyebrows and smile.

But don't students get totally drunk? Leaving me as the adult responsible? Once or twice, yes, someone needed help getting home. And I know students overdo it at the *nijikai*, the after-party they often head to. On our shared LINE app, they post photos of a classmate or two passed out on an all-night karaoke bar bench. It's hard not to laugh, but I find students rarely overindulge. Not as much as I did anyway. For them, drinking as an escape or limit-testing is not the point—being together is.

More than anything, students talk about their futures, and once job-hunting starts in their fourth year, that's all they talk about. They ask me a lot of questions about why I became a teacher. Was it the same when I was young? No. Did I ever work in a company? No. Whether my experience applies or not may not be the point. Sharing attitudes, anecdotes, and advice helps them think it all through. Maybe that's all a university education ever does—help think things through.

We always talk in English. They ask many questions about how to study too, but in a different way than in class, where they tend not to ask many questions. In that sense, our *nomikai* bridges the gap between school and life in ways I don't always grasp. Having moved between the two realms all my life, I often forget how hard it is to take something learned at school and apply it in the real world. University learning usually stops before the point of contact.

Maybe that's because all the fun gets excised from school learning. Classrooms in Japan are generally set up as places for serious, self-conscious attendance to policies and rules. But *nomikai* break that up. I can always bullshit the students in class. I have the whole edifice of the university behind me. But over a glass of beer, I find it hard to bullshit them at all. Being with them there restores the honesty needed for genuine understanding.

The talk crammed into our two hours at the *izakaya* involves more subtlety and individuality than inside the classroom. They bring themselves to the conversation instead of acting like cardboard cutout students. In a casual setting, they can reveal who they are. The mousy girl who blushes in class is mature and experienced. The class clown is desperate to succeed. The always-prepared student gets flustered about what to say. When things become unscripted, unconstrained, and de-centered, we all have to interact with richer dimensions of ourselves.

That lets me see them as complete, rounded people and helps me interact with them more fully. It makes me teach with greater sensitivity. After sounding out the depths—and shallows—of students, I am reminded that school is just one thing they do, the most important thing for some, less so for others. Talking without school constraints lets us get down to root causes—why they are studying, how they view their work, where they are coming from, and where they want to go.

Shouldn't I know this from the classroom? I should, maybe, but even after years of teaching, I usually can't see past their in-class manner. Does that matter? It does to me. I don't like teaching based on guesswork or some imagined picture of who is there and what should happen. I want to see what can really happen by knowing the missing pieces that bring the larger picture into focus. It enables me to map out larger contexts and higher goals for them. It helps me encourage their ambitions and bolster their confidence.

Of course, that happens inside the classroom too, but outside school, we're repositioned into a much larger frame. Sitting there with them around a table, passing plates and glasses back and forth, is very different from standing in the front of the classroom where I can direct the proceedings. There's no micromanaging a *nomikai* chat.

That's especially important for a literature seminar because the frame for literature is, after all, a huge one—life itself. Literary study can sometimes, unfortunately, become stifling, like looking at wild animals trapped in a zoo. A little sign is hung in front of the novel, film, or short story, and we're looking in, not looking through or looking out. I like being outside the university for just that reason. It ups the stakes for what we do in class. Students and I start looking at stories and language as a human construction, an essential part of life, rather than feeling removed from it for dissection.

As we eat and drink, change seats, zip through discussion topics, laugh, and let loose, at some point, we all start speaking from the heart. It's a relief not to be a teacher for a while, to return to what I like best about the world, what I loved from when I was in college—traveling, talking, and telling stories. I become a human being visiting Japan, a traveler traveling, not a teacher toeing the university line.

At some point, when imbibing slows down and our two hours are almost over, students click into fully honest mode. That gives me a chance to speak from the heart. They let emotions come out, and so do I. Reserve and restraint are values teachers put on like jackets, but they are good ones to set aside from time to time. Jackets become straitjackets all too easily.

When the students tell the story of their studies from their point of view, emotion reenters the proceedings. Things can get dry and distant inside even the most dynamic classroom because everyone tries to be intelligent, not passionate. But at *nomikai*, all of us can reveal frustrations, pleasures, joys, successes, and feared failures. When that happens, like in a good story, feeling subverts intellect.

These *nomikai* are like the subtext of a story, hidden until you get it. They prove William James's observation that "We learn to swim during the winter and to skate during the summer." It's the downtime that makes the uptime click. To hear students' stories of successful job-hunting, of success at getting a part in a student play, of losing their mother to cancer but making the dean's list studying abroad, of deciding to take a year off for work-study—all of that makes the stories in class make more sense.

It would be ironic if we only studied literary and cinematic stories in class but made no attempt to share our own. I want them to see the omnipresence of stories and their power to explain and shape our lives. Without sharing a story, we don't truly live it or even understand it.

And selfishly, I get to see their lives, and through the story of their lives, I see Japan. They get what Pierre Bourdieu called "cultural capital," and I get savvier about Japan and how to teach. But more than anything, talking helps restore honesty, emotionality, and joy, which are, after all, the core values of all literature. It certainly helps keep me from being a noun—the teacher—and helps me remain in verb form—teaching. I'm grateful for that.

At the end of the *nomikai*, we always stop for a photo outside the *izakaya*, a moment of still precision, asking some passerby or wait staff to take a picture with all of us together. We pose and let the camera do its work, and then we return to the flow of our lives, heading for different trains and our different stories.

But for a couple of hours, inside that single last photo, we've packed our hopes, frustrations, misunderstandings, and energies—a shared chapter of our stories—and we're all the better for it—wiser, more trusting, and more humane.

Rights in the Matter

Over this damp grave I speak the words of my love:
I, with no rights in this matter,
Neither father nor lover.
"Elegy for Jane (My student, thrown by a horse)"
Theodore Roethke (1953)

The first time one of my students died, it caught me so unaware I didn't have time to react. The chairperson of my department stopped me on the stairs and told me the news. My mind flew back to my last conversation with her in my office, and then my mind scattered in all directions—practicalities, confusions, thoughts, whens, ifs, and could-I-haves. I went to the student affairs office for directions to the funeral service at the crematorium in western Tokyo.

At the funeral hall, I spoke with her father, acting as a representative of the university that would be—was—her final social connection, her last institution on earth. I offered him my few Japanese words of consolation and sat down with her classmates, their heads bowed and pale, all dressed in black. Many of them I knew, though I didn't know they had been her friends. But then, what did I know of her life? Almost nothing.

She had been writing her graduation thesis on American architecture and had taken a trip to Chicago to photograph buildings there. She was compact and energetic, her feet barely touching the floor when she sat in a chair in my office, and full of energy, bouncing like a much younger girl. She was unbelievably cute, with dimples that made you smile back. She was finding her voice in English to talk about her thesis and her dreams after graduation, as well as more study and travel. She was more hesitant than most other students at the private university in the middle of Tokyo, but every student was hesitant in some way.

Photos of her taken by her boyfriend punctuated the flowers lining the funeral hall. The poses felt alive. She was just as striking in black and white and two dimensions, but I had to look away. As the ceremony began, I tried to be calm and strong for the other students, for the family, and for myself.

At the end of the incense lighting and chanting, her father gave a short speech, one of the most impressive acts I've ever witnessed. Though as a teacher, I talked in front of people all the time, I could never be half that strong. What could be harder than to speak at your own daughter's funeral?

As the family slowly, numbly, pushed her open casket down the center aisle towards the furnace, the potent scent of incense and flowers drained the blood from my head, and I had to breathe through my mouth. I looked, looked away, looked, away. Students stepped up to the casket to drop in flowers, cards, books, and photos on top of her small body. They touched the casket and covered their face with both hands, shaking, shocked, doubling over, folded in half by grief. The family pushed her body down the silent hall.

And then she was gone.

I gathered the students, and we struggled into our heavy black coats and out to the bus and the train station. One student, silent as we rode on the bus, burst into tears after a few stops on the train. Everyone around us on the train eyed us, sympathetic to what was obvious—a student had died far too young. I held his elbow to steady him, and another student took his arm from the other side as tears dripped to the floor. We swayed along on the crowded train, joined in grief.

I wondered if I could have done better by being closer in some way, mentoring, helping more, and advising her more fully and more personably. Did I not ask her the right question? Not say the right thing? I never thought I acted cold or removed, but my confusion seemed to mark the distance I kept from students. What was I supposed to feel? Where does a professor fit into the life of a student? I had no idea. This wasn't about me, but then again, it was. It was about everyone. University meant the universe, all of it.

I had never imposed strict rules of engagement like some of my colleagues—demanding to be called "professor," refusing to listen to private problems, and concealing my own life. I'd always given out my email, joined LINE groups, friended on Facebook, and coughed up stories of my youthful mistakes. I invited my seminar students to my home for barbecues, figuring that for Japanese students, the experience of dealing with a foreigner was part of their education.

I always found it fascinating to talk with students as human beings. Academic aloofness might seem dignified, but to me, it was boring. I liked knowing their lives outside the classroom. Now, I knew one of their deaths.

Buddhist funeral rituals often involve distributing salt in a small envelope to purify oneself ritually. After her funeral, instead of throwing the salt in front of my door as I was supposed to, I placed the envelope on the bookshelf over my office desk—a reminder to maybe not be so pure. Instead, I wanted to be less guarded and more human. I tried to pay better attention and not be afraid of knowing students as individuals and letting them know me.

The second student, who died several years later, had been easier to get to know because he was interested in things I loved—rock music, Beat Generation writers, and stand-up comedy. He had this way of getting deeply into the class materials while staying indifferent to the concerns of most students—job hunting, fashion, boyfriends/girlfriends, and Disney. He was, like I had been, a bit of an outsider.

Like me, his difference from other students came less from distance to schoolwork than closeness to life outside school. He worked, had friends, performed, read non-required books, and went to concerts—my same itinerary as when I was a student. I lent him books and DVDs and shared advice on what to read and watch and where to travel in America, trying to keep his curiosity stoked and fed.

At the service, I met his seminar classmates at the train station and bumped into some of his acting and comedy friends, whom I had informed about his death. We rode together to the crematorium, located inconveniently far from the station—an inconvenience that allowed us a few, insufficiently few, moments to prepare ourselves.

After signing in, I expressed my condolences to the family. His father led me right into the hall and up to the open casket. I had responded to the inner vitality in my student so much over the three years he took classes with me that I started to talk with him in my head as I looked at his face below the glass. But the fact of his face there told me he wasn't going to jump up like some ironic practical joke in the films he watched. He was not going to America to travel or study again. He was not going to graduate school. He was not going to finish his graduation thesis on stand-up comedy. He was dead.

For most of the other seminar students, this was their first experience of a peer's death. I didn't want to tell them that it never gets better, that it's always painful, consistently awful, and that the images, feelings, regrets, and anxieties linger in your head for years and years and never disappear. It's not something you get better at. Death is when life moves on before it can be understood.

The ceremony was lengthy because so many people came. Towards the end, as the casket rolled past, we stood in two lines, memories and feelings roiling inside us. In our funeral clothes, we all looked much the same in the face of death—like we all were part of one big black eye. We were a black hole of feelings. The casket was filled with flowers and mementos as his family, classmates, and friends wailed loudly, forcefully, and unceasingly. The family rolled him away, and we watched him go.

Afterward, the students and I lingered outside the hall by a corkboard covered in photos from his life. We were all of us somewhere in the photos with him—at parties, last class days, workplaces, stages, selfies. We walked back and forth in front of the corkboard, looking at him, ourselves, his friends, his places, his experiences, the brevity of his life. And as we looked back and forth, reluctant to leave, part of us, part of him, was dying still. His interests were so similar to mine that I felt a bit of myself die.

As I stood waiting for the bus back to the station with the students, I asked them what they had been doing in the half-year since they'd graduated. Their seminar had finished the April before, though he had stayed for a fifth year, acting as a TA and planning for grad school.

The students in his seminar mainly talked about work and how hard it was to be a *shakaijin*, a working member of society. It wasn't just getting up early every day or working late. It was more the difficulty of working with other people. One woman had quit already. Another said she would work for two years and then return to school if she could. Some seemed satisfied, others not very.

They reminded me that as a professor at a Japanese university, most of my interactions and relationships are scripted. But not all. It's the "not all" part that demands energy, time, thought, and emotion. As a professor of literature, what comes up in classroom discussions again and again is emotion and ethics, feelings and decisions.

That's what stories are—practice runs at life's big, mean questions. At some point in most of my classes, we list the great themes of the novels on the board, and students are always good at shouting them out. They know them already. When death comes up in class, it always feels distant and abstract, a thought more than a feeling, a word on the board. Knowing from stories and knowing from life are two banks of the same river.

The novels we read in that seminar were little help in the face of real death. Isn't it the funeral of a student, a classmate, a friend, or a relative that literature *should* help us with? It's supposed to help us understand the nature of the world. It ought to give us some warning of what's up ahead. We might not all be Hamlet, but we are all surrounded by friends and enemies, poisons and swords, truths and lies, and whispering ghosts on the parapets. We all hesitate to act and crave direction. We want explanations but rarely get them. But as the art critic and novelist John Berger said, "If every event which occurred could be given a name, there would be no need for stories."

Teachers often joke about being eternal students, always learning more from the people we teach than we give to them. The lessons I usually get from my students vary from insights into human character and youth's perennial frustrations and procrastinations to decisions on jobs and life directions. I didn't like being taught about the core fact of our existence—its end.

Theodore Roethke's poem came to mind when I frantically re-read the email informing me of his death. I checked to be sure they meant him, called the university office to confirm, and then, unsure of what to say to her, I called his mother to offer what I hoped would be consoling words, stumbling over the correct phrases in Japanese. The poem came to me, not word for word, but in pieces. After the funeral, I searched for it online.

I first read Roethke's poem in an old anthology from which I borrowed material for classes when I started teaching. It was written for a student who died while Roethke was teaching at an East Coast girls' school. I didn't have a copy of the anthology any longer, but I remembered the painting on the cover by Magritte, "The False Eye." It shows a giant black dot in the middle of a cloud-filled blue sky, an eyelid lining the inside of the frame, perceiver and perceived reversed.

In his elegiac poem, Roethke used the word "love" to describe his feelings as he stood at the student's grave. But that was in a different, more innocent time. The 1950s was long before that word became coded as inappropriate for workplace relationships and re-categorized as something to be avoided. Never saying that became a safeguard against abuse and harassment in relationships of power. Fair enough.

But until an acceptably politically correct word comes along, one sanctioned by institutions, that fits all the legal and professional demands of the current world, I think it will do to sum up the flow of feelings that made these deaths so tragic. That makes any untimely death tragic. The same set of tangled, unnamable feelings makes teaching a joy the rest of the time—for graduations, parties, job acceptance, a high grade, or well-done work. Commiseration and celebration even out over time.

After the funeral, I reread Roethke's poem alone in my office. I looked out my window at the lights of Tokyo in the distance. Then I printed out the poem in a tight, sharp font, cut away the white space around the words, and stuck it with a magnet onto the bookshelf over my desk below the small envelope of salt from the first funeral, in the half-empty place where I store my hidden feelings about teaching.

Context for My Outrage

"Outrage" was never a word that came up in my graduate school courses. It doesn't come up in any of the books I read on pedagogy or the purpose of university, on literature or liberal arts. It's not even a word that I use very often. But my students showed me what it meant by what they went through after they graduated—the women especially. As much as the academic pedagogy books on my shelves, my students' stories pushed me to rethink my teaching.

Aya's story

Aya got a job with a travel company, which fit her well. Her English was good, and she was a hard worker, but not ambitious, or seemingly not. Aya and a few other students met me at a wine bar. She said she'd come to love wine after going to Oregon on a wine tour, a perk of her job. Tourist agencies in America invited Japanese agents to see the tours, so she'd visited America many times since graduation.

We talked a lot that night, all the students sharing their stories about work and twenty-something life. As the wine soaked in, the students, predictably, talked more freely. Aya said she didn't like her tourist agency because she did all the work.

I asked, "All the work?" Yes, I run the office, she said, and the other students, all women, laughed. It was the same at their jobs. Her boss was nice, she explained but didn't do much. I said, "Don't tell me...(Famous) University?" "No, (Equally Famous) University." We all laughed.

She explained that her boss, a man only a couple of years

older, just sat there all day saying yes or no to whatever she took to him. Tourist agencies in America would call with promotional opportunities, and she would talk with them, explaining that her boss—the head of the North America tour section for a large travel bureau—could not speak English.

She started to understand that this guy from a prestigious university—or someone like him—was going to be in charge forever. She was doing *his* work for *him*, and he was getting the credit and a higher salary. She knew that because she did the accounts as well.

She was in the right job, but he was not. But the system was set up that way, so she put up with it for several years because she was improving her English and going on great tours all over America. Those places were running out, though, along with her patience. I felt impatient just listening to her. I felt irritated at her situation and irritated she wasn't more irritated, though I knew she didn't even know how to articulate her frustration.

Yuka's story

Yuka was one of the best students I've ever taught. She was one of those students you don't teach—you step aside and wave them forward. She received four A+ grades from me in one semester. The demanding classes all in English didn't bother her. She relished the challenge. I was disappointed when she ended up in the personnel department of a mid-sized, traditional company, but she seemed OK with it.

She sent messages about everything she was doing, and it sounded like she was coming out of her shell. She had been a shy student, but giving presentations at schools and conducting interviews with prospective employees gave her newfound confidence. She didn't use English at her job, but she was learning new skills. Plus, she told me the company was expanding overseas, and she could maybe work in America.

It turned out the expansion wasn't for everyone. The male employees hired at the same time--or after her—started getting sent abroad. The men weren't sent to work but to study English. And yet, Yuka's English didn't need any brushing up. Why, she asked her boss, were they getting sent abroad, but not her?

He didn't say directly, but the reason was clear. She was the only woman in the personnel section. Then, things got worse.

The male employees sent abroad to study had to write essays in English. Only they couldn't. So, they sent those assignments back to the section chief, who assigned the essays to Yuka. Stuck in Tokyo, with no chance to work abroad, she had to write essays for the men who had been sent abroad!

The final insult happened one day when she was talking with a section chief about the qualifications for a new position. She took down his requirements and noted there were always many women at the recruitment fairs. "*Josei dame!*" "Women, no way!" the section chief shouted. At that moment, her future at that company became obvious.

I could only listen. This marvelous student, so full of promise and accomplished in English, was given dull work in a constrained and unfair environment. She couldn't complain because she was in human resources—the place to complain to.

I felt angrier than she did. That section chief's outlook, in fact, her whole company's outlook, was not just insulting *her* as a woman and as an individual. He was insulting the entire set of values, the whole four years of study that was *my* work. Yuka worked hard on her English, studied abroad, and did everything right. She had excelled at school but was held back at work. It was outrageous.

Mika's story

Mika emailed me to ask if she could stop by my office. For several years, she'd been a *shakaijin*, that strange Japanese term meaning literally "social people," but used for people who are no longer students but working. She was thinking of going back to graduate school. When she came to my office, we went over application procedures, standardized tests, and how to craft a good personal essay. She wanted to do translation studies.

That seemed perfect for her because after graduation, she'd been working in a commodity company that made purchases in real time—in English. It was a dream job for most English majors, so I asked her why she wanted to change. She explained that despite the excitement of working in English with brokers all over the world, she needed a change. We got on with the application process. She pulled the materials into order, and we emailed back and forth about the application.

Finally, she was accepted into several translation programs in the UK. It was success on success. But, somehow, she didn't seem so pleased. Then, the real reason for quitting came out.

Mika told me she was quitting because her boss wouldn't stop sending her messages and making comments. What kind of comments? I asked. About sex, she said. Ah, I said, my hackles raised.

When she rebuffed him, he blamed her for small things

and gave her more work. She was already doing most of the work since her boss didn't speak English. In a few years, she had learned how to buy, sell, import, and export commodities, but always needed his OK in Japanese for even the smallest trade. He harassed her that way too.

She told me that after applying to graduate school, she fell apart one day at work. Her boss's harassment became too much. One morning, she ran into a toilet stall and could not stop crying. The human resources people rescued her, and she spilled the entire story in a conference room.

The HR people sent her home for a few days' rest, and, in the meantime, they started talking to other women who had transferred out of that section. They told similar stories. In the time it took for her to get into graduate school, her boss had been fired.

Great, I said, as she both laughed and cried in my office. You were tough, I told her, but inside I was seething. I was disgusted with Japanese workplaces and angry at the horrible situation she'd been in. Was this the government's so-called *womenomics*?

My story

What could I have done to make things better for these students? As a male teacher teaching female students, how could I have wised them up to what awaited after graduation? Were the forces outside the university too strong to be countered by a teacher? Or was that just how things were—unfair and unjust?

In some ways, of course, it's not my responsibility. I could shuck it off and not worry about anything beyond the classroom walls. I could leave all thoughts of students' private lives at the gate to the university. I could take a graduation photo with them and get back to focusing on "my job," "my research," and "my writing." After all, a couple weeks after graduation, new students would arrive, and the cycle would start again.

However, hearing their experiences changed my view of what teaching literature and film in English was all about. The disconnect between literature study, which is supposed to be about life, and actual life was a chasm I hadn't yet bridged as a teacher, mentor, writer, or person.

Or maybe I was looking at it the wrong way. If they had not studied literature, they would have been even worse off. Maybe literature presented conflicts and resolutions in ways that helped them find similar patterns in their lives. I wondered if studying characters in conflict, the engine of stories, energized them to take action.

Instead of obedience and silent suffering, they had developed a sense of irony. That sense of irony provided the needed distance from which to view the problem and find the footing to handle it. I wondered how I could teach that better. Grad school theories and criticism led me away from that kind of analysis. That wasn't bad, but it wasn't helpful.

I always gave my students lists of questions to help them negotiate reading, analyzing, and discussing stories, but I added more questions on the emotions and conflicts in the stories. I wanted them to see that themes, symbols, characters, conflicts, and points of view are not just in-school games, not just blanks to fill in. They are the very patterns in which people and the world exist. Was I failing at that? or was it trickier than I'd imagined?

Understanding stories is practice for understanding oneself inside one's own story, but it's also more than that. It's a step towards finding equilibrium in the face of frustrating, unfair realities. Stories provide a mental space to develop the mindset and abilities to change, leave, or fight back and to do it with understanding.

Knowing students' post-graduation lives pushed my teaching into a larger context. I started to understand that the classroom had been too confined by the university's boundaries. I'd let it be confined. It was missing lived experience.

If I couldn't figure out how to coax literature closer to life, it wouldn't ever be much help tangling with practical issues of survival, growth, and threat. If literature didn't expand my viewing frame, it wouldn't expand theirs. It wasn't them that was too narrow; it was me.

What struck me most about their post-university stories was how deeply they felt about them. That was what was missing from my class. It was as if sharp, intense emotion—its presence, analysis, and understanding—had been banned from my classroom, repressed in the curriculum, and kept hidden in our hearts. Feeling was more than just a missing element of the class—it was what students and I needed most. It was what literature most had to offer.

So, the first immediate challenge to expand my teaching frame was handling emotion—the ingredient most often left out of most academic courses. It's easy to teach bloodlessly, without any feeling. It makes things go smoothly. It keeps things tidy. It's easier to grade. But it's a disservice to students not to focus on the tangle of complex emotions and painful situations in literature as a preparation for what they will encounter after graduation, not just at work, but in life.

Of course, everyone who works has emotional conflicts, and not everything fits into a meaningful narrative.

Literature is no panacea. Other students have told me unbelievable tales of ending up in jobs requiring them to clean the office toilet every morning or work through lunch breaks. Overtime is a given. Others ended up in disastrous retail positions with lazy or maniacal bosses. Others worked until they collapsed and had to quit to recover.

Their tales paint a grim picture of Japanese working society. Literature alone could not provide enough emotional armor, self-awareness, people skills, or humor to handle all that. But I started to feel more deeply that it would help.

In the end, after her harassing boss was fired, Mika waited it out at her company and finally got posted abroad to the same position, but in London. Yuka quit her company and found a position at a European consulate, where she uses English daily. Aya quit her travel agency and went to graduate school in Canada to get a degree in business.

I'd like to see where their male bosses end up after ten or twenty years, compared to what my students will achieve. I know how their stories will turn out, even if I don't know the exact ending. Literature, after all, is good about endings. In literature, as in life, outrage doesn't last forever.

Tears for English

I am talking to Junko, a fourth-year student, in my office. She tells me she will not be able to finish her senior graduation paper, and I'm listening as closely as possible.

"It's OK," I tell her. You worked hard for four years, and now you can't finish one paper. Don't worry about it." The paper is not required for graduation. It's an extra challenge that I encourage students to take, but don't sweat if they don't finish.

"Yes," Junko says, "I know, but I really wanted to finish this. It's important to me, but I started too late. I know not to start late, but I did it anyway." Her face starts to get drawn and tight, far from her usual pleasant look. She starts to explain why, and I listen to her extremely good English try to wrap itself around the bulky shape of excuses and self-criticisms.

She starts to list the reasons: her father got sick, so she went back to her hometown; she had to look for a job, which didn't go well at first; she got sick and went to the doctor; and, of course, she started too late and chose a too-broad topic. She couldn't organize her time. She couldn't read enough. It was the usual suspects, the typical litany.

"I know," I tell her. "It's OK. You don't need the credit to graduate, so why worry so much?" But of course, as often happens, I'm missing the point.

Junko starts to cry, and tears pour out. "It's like I didn't learn anything at all in four years!" she moans. "I wanted to write this graduation paper to show myself I could do it. But I just couldn't finish. I wrote some but couldn't get it to come together!" Then, she crumples into sobs, and I reach for the tissues that I keep on my desk for just these moments.

Another weeping student, I think to myself. I pull out tissue after tissue and drag the wastepaper can over so she can throw out the used tissues without having to stop crying to apologize for handing the wet tissues to me to throw out. I've been here before.

I sit quietly to let her cry it out for a few minutes, but she continues wave after wave of uncontrollable sobs. As the pile of tissues grows in the trash can, she finally slows enough to catch her breath. I explain a few points to her about studying, language, writing, and life. She's listening as if for the first time. It's as if she had to weep before she could listen, to clear out the feeling to make room for understanding.

"I failed quite a few classes myself," I tell her.

She looks up with wet, red eyes. "You did?"

"And I survived. I took a few classes and didn't finish them. Once, I even walked out of a creative writing class, I got so angry at the teacher."

She looks at me.

I say, "You probably have better reasons than I did! I was just sick of it all."

She looks at me and then crumples the tissues in her hands. "I always tried to be such a good student."

"You are a good student."

"I'm sick of being good."

I try not to laugh. I don't want to laugh because it's ridiculous, though it is. I want to laugh because I know exactly how she feels. It's how many students feel, and it messes them up.

Junko lets out a big breath, looks at the wet tissues in her hand, and starts to come back to herself. After another breath or two, she recomposes herself. Of course, what I tell her is nothing different than what I have already said and no different than what I *do* in the classroom. But of course, my tone of voice is different after her weeping. She's made me remember how overwhelming these worries and sufferings can be.

This same scene repeats itself in my office every year. Most students do not cry in the teacher's office, but those who do, trust me—or trust the world. They need to share their feelings and ask me if it is OK that they feel so strongly about studying English and studying in general. It's a question they should ask, but don't know how to ask, so they almost always ask it too late.

I assured her, like I do all the students, that it is OK to suffer over wanting to do something well. There's no other way to do things well than through suffering. Sometimes, students have serious problems in their lives, and I've often listened as they cry or complain about a myriad of troubling issues. But for my students in the English Department, English is what they take pride in and what they feel bad about when they do not do it right.

I admire these students' passion and their capacity for profound feelings. Most classes do not allow time for feeling and emotion, though learning a language is a highly emotional undertaking, more so when a single path is chosen and must be followed. Students can't make as many changes to their trajectory as in some countries. On top of this, most students store all their feelings in some hidden part of themselves, sealed away from the intellectual and academic approach of studying English at school. They are serious and mature, but they wear themselves out.

However, from time to time, those suppressed feelings explode and it all comes pouring out in a rush of tears. Students all over the world cry, but for Japanese students, studying English is a powerful, deeply felt experience that binds up a range of feelings, worries, anxieties, confusions, and desires.

For many students, English becomes central to their identity. It's the one thing they do well. But it's more than that. Studying English forms a large part of their maturing into their self-created identity, not the one given to them. They look to the future when they can be bilingual and use English in the international workplace. They want to be a global person. It's a way of escaping what they view as the constraints of being monolingual in a city like Tokyo, which is becoming more multinational by the day. They fear they'll be left out.

The students know they can only participate in Tokyo's global side if they speak another language. This puts positive pressure on them most of the time, but it can become too much when they falter. It's not just English study—it's how they will lead their lives in a complex city. Others want a career at a company with non-Japanese colleagues. Others want to keep learning. And still others want to live differently, to open themselves to the world.

So, they build their hopes on English as a springboard to what they see as the exciting side of Tokyo's complexity—the English-speaking side. Their dreams are of a life in Tokyo, speaking Japanese and English, with a balance of language, work, thinking, and living that is global and local in the perfect blend. It's the dream of the big city that happens in every country, but in Japan, the dream is a pressurized one.

To achieve that dream, students learn English in a series of steps that require grinding dedication. Schools emphasize perfection, perfect pronunciation, perfect grammar, memorized speeches, and an ever-higher TOEFL score. The string of tightly structured exams wears them out. They translate in their minds and can't perform directly in English without using Japanese first.

Looking ahead, they become frustrated when they stumble at actually using English. They find it hard to leap from the grammar- and test-based approach to language study and the freer use of the language. They know they have to speak in English, write emails abroad, and attend meetings with foreigners whose command of English might be better than theirs. All of that pressures them and can push them to the breaking, or crying, point.

Much of the reason for crying is frustration and a bit of anger, though the anger is not always directed at any one thing. The system has let them down, with an insufficient curriculum and odd pressures to get a job, whatever the TOEFL score. Some students become disillusioned with the educational system, but most become disappointed in themselves. Instead of saying the system failed them, they despair at not having done things perfectly.

Like any other human undertaking, learning a language involves emotional sacrifice. Psychic energy is bound up with the many activities language learning requires. Teachers and learners try to look away from the emotional side of learning, mainly because it's so messy. Focusing on drills, skills, tasks, homework, and testable elements is easier. The system has failed them by hermetically sealing them in tasks that exclude human emotion.

The textbooks most students use are dry and bland. That's why I find the stories in novels and films, the metaphors of poetry and song lyrics, the imagination-stirring effect of art, and other aspects of culture to be much better content for students. Content with emotion allows for attachment. Otherwise, it's like math: connect the two vocabulary items, input the correct grammatical pattern, and discuss something dull and unimportant, but discuss it correctly.

The true learning of a language always involves a great deal of emotional processing. Classes in the language, maybe more than any other subject, need to establish an environment where emotions can be tapped, even indirectly, as a source of energy and accepted as a natural part of the process. What usually happens, though, is language is presented by textbooks and teachers as a logical, rational undertaking. Some students learn that way, but only up to a point.

Below the surface of every great language learner is a huge storehouse of deeply felt and closely involved feelings. It is not the indifferent students who cry in my office—it's the passionate ones. I tell Junko that and try to get her to understand. She's not crying because of her failure to finish her graduation thesis. She's crying because English means so much to her. It's at the core of who she is and who she wants to be.

The students who collapse in cascades of tears always profusely apologize. They feel ashamed that they cannot control themselves, but I tell them their crying shows they care deeply. Caring deeply always hurts more, but it means more too. My great fear is not that students care too much but care too little—or not at all.

I always feel re-humanized after these crying sessions. Maybe that's selfish, but it resets me and reminds me I'm dealing with human beings—ones in process—who take their studies seriously, even when they don't know quite how to do that. Students often feign indifference, which makes it easy to respond in kind. Teachers often hide behind rational fronts to construct defenses against the anxiety and emotion of just being with human beings in their complexity. Like Tokyoites in general, they pretend not to care sometimes, but that is only a defense against the depth of their caring.

The hardest thing I do as a teacher is to listen to their emotional outpourings. There was no class about that at graduate school. I'm thankful when students push me into the emotional terrain I often circumnavigate. It's like a remedial class in the reality of human beings and what they consider important. Behind the big city cool is a deep pool of feeling.

Learning goes to the very core of our human nature. That is a truth worth crying over, one that my students teach me about again and again with their tears. When I see the serious faces on the train or on the streets of Tokyo, I know they've cried too.

Before I Taught a Poem I'd Ask to Know

In my "Survey of American Literature" class, I've always enjoyed reading student responses. Typically, students respond with the smooth predictability of Japanese mass education. When we read poems written by women, students tell me how women are oppressed. When we read an e.e. cummings poem, they love the child-like play of language. An excerpt from Kerouac brings out their wanderlust, and studying anti-war songs brings the inevitable: "War is bad."

I read their responses on the train home or later that evening and give them feedback with the teacherly confidence most professors acquire. I teach. Students learn. Done.

But once a semester, that gets undone. It always happens with Robert Frost's well-known, often-taught poem, "Mending Wall." It's a simple (I thought) poem about walls and neighbors. I chose it because it is accessible and a good re-read. But what I get from students confuses and unsettles me. To paraphrase Frost, something there is that doesn't love a teacher's walls, that wants them down.

My high school English classroom in Kansas had a poster on the wall of Frost's craggy, kindly face next to a quote from the poem, "Before I built a wall, I'd ask to know." I took the poem as a basic precept for venturing into the world. Don't be afraid to question things or take things apart. I took walls as something to spend my life breaking down. I wanted a wall-less life. And mostly, I got one. I traveled, married, worked, and befriended far beyond the walls of my youth.

But my students don't always read the poem like I do. They often praise walls, appreciate them, and argue in favor of their necessity. I mean, praise walls? I can't believe it. For me, the poem preached the gospel of freedom. Embrace the other in honest rapport. But for some students, the poem is a reminder to be wary. They argue for staying distant, reserved, and quiet.

The plainspoken neighborliness of the flat plains of Kansas, where I grew up, has a much shorter legacy than that of the intricate relations and hierarchies of Japanese society. Were the students and I, on opposite sides of the poem's wall, acting out some archetypal differences? Was this some culture clash or just a different set of personal readings?

I give my students a choice of questions to discuss and write about.

1. How is the neighbor's character different from the narrator's? Which do you like better?

2. Which saying do you agree with more: "Something there is that doesn't love a wall" OR "Good fences make good neighbors"?

3. What kind of walls do you have in your life? What do you build your "walls" with?

Everyone agrees on the first question. They dislike the neighbor, "an old-stone savage armed," who "moves in darkness" and will not "go behind his father's saying." He's a dull sod, unthinking, conservative, and unimaginative. They like the narrator, a clever wordsmith who questions, jokes, and thinks broadly. It's obvious who the good guy is.

Students also leap in on the third question, offering laments about the walls surrounding them—language, family, school, their shyness, and chronic indecision. They have a lot of walls and seem practiced at cataloging them.

However, with the second question, more than half side with the saying of the neighbor, "Good fences make good neighbors." The line is repeated twice in the poem, as is the opposing idea, "Something there is that doesn't love a wall." When asked to choose, most favor replacing the fallen boulders to re-build the wall. That always stuns me.

Of course, some students translate the neighbor's saying into Japanese and then back to English. They find 親しき仲にも礼儀あり (*Shitashiki naka nimo reigi ari*) on the internet and copy-paste the re-translation, "There is courtesy even among close friends." That doesn't sound too bad, but it's different from the neighbor in the poem who "will not go behind his father's saying." This ping-pong of meanings moves farther from the poem, not into it.

Overall, I have to admit students make pretty good arguments for walls. They write:

We tend to make the wall for people we meet for the first time and seniors, because if we interact with them with no walls, that's a rude behavior, and maybe breaks the relationship between us. So, people use honorific as a wall of respect.

I think "fences" appears in this saying as appropriate distances or rules like courtesy in relationship.

I think a good relationship needs appropriate distance. When you get too close to someone, you start seeing negative sides to their personality. I think that giving space can maintain a better relationship.

I don't think it's always a good idea to reveal everything about yourself to someone. In my opinion, a good sense of distance builds a good relationship because we don't expose everything about ourselves, even to those who are close.

I agree with "Good fences makes good neighbors" because most Japanese people like to keep distance with others especially strangers or people who they do not know well. I have heard that there is culture that people talk to each other even they do not know each other in other country. However, people do not like talking to strangers in Japan.

No matter how close we are, there are some things we never want to be known or stepped into. And if we cross that borderline of not wanting to be trespassed, it could lead to a fight. That is why I think it is very important to draw the line of the wall from the beginning.

I can sense students articulating an awareness of the delicate structure of relationships. I'm impressed with their search for a more refined and manageable way of interacting. Maybe Japanese relationships really are more complex, but I just can't see that from my American side of the wall.

I'm always careful to tell them that with literature, there are no "right" answers. And yet, there must be better or worse answers. This is not a poem about baseball or bicycles. It's about human relationships, types of characters, ways of living in the world, working with others, and about how we choose to distance ourselves or let barriers fall. Like the narrator in the poem, I want them to at least wonder, "Why do walls make good neighbors?"

But maybe it is me who is culture-bound. I don't want to judge their responses from my American point of view, but I feel exasperated at their closed-in-ness. I've always seen literature as a liberating force, not a guide to manners. Isn't there some Platonic ideal of wall-less-ness? Or is that my American fantasy of freedom? Maybe my overweening belief in the rightness of always connecting stops me from seeing the other side.

Some students, of course, hate walls and write about how confining they are. Like me, they long to get beyond them. I nod in smug satisfaction at the similarity of our thoughts. But I also stop to wonder about the wall-loving students. Are they conservative, afraid-of-the-world types, too shy to speak up in class? Are they just answering what they thought was the expected answer, the safe reply? Are they building a wall to protect their walls? Am I?

The wall-loving students seem to be searching for walls that prevent them from being imposed on and could strand them in a field of obligations. Walls in dense Asian cities mean something very different than in New England's pine forests and apple orchards. In the densely packed cities of Tokyo and Yokohama, walls are a relief from the constant stream of people, choices, and demands. When people live close by, walls become a shield from the surrounding eyes, safeguarding independence and protecting privacy.

At nineteen or twenty years old, students need to try out new relationships and make tough decisions for themselves. Maybe a little distancing helps with that, shielding them from failure or shame and allowing them a moment to think before engaging.

But then I also think they're unwilling to step outside their safe confines and confront the world. Japanese students seem reluctant to open up and are way too comfortable staying walled inside themselves. Their walls are cemented by the craving for comfort. Don't they want to see what would happen on the other side? With all those walls, how do they ever open up to bigger ideas, friendships, action, and love?

Then again, maybe I've been using the poem as an elaborate, rather adolescent, defense for all my own wall-jumping. Perhaps I need to examine my walls more closely. I tend to leave too many boulders behind. The students seem to focus on building the right walls, an oddly mature insight, while I've always reveled in the belief that "something there is that doesn't love a wall, that wants it down" is better.

I realize now that having students as neighbors in learning, language, and literature involves shifting the focus from the wall to the mending, from the static singularity of words on a page to multiple, fluid meanings. When that something that wants the wall down gets it down, then what's left is just the meeting there. I've started to think that it's that moment of meeting, of talking and working that is the point of the poem, not the wall.

Reading the poem with students every semester at "spring mending-time" brings the students to the wall for the first time and me for the umpteenth time. Like the poem's two characters, "On a day we meet to walk the line/And set the wall between us once again." Together, we pick up the boulders—of words, questions, reactions, and discoveries—and set them gently into place. It's a re-building, done together.

The tricky thing is the dual focus—building up and breaking down—two parts of the same process. Literature positions readers inside and outside, as in a dream, constructing meanings in one place and taking apart meanings in another. Poems can get us to think and talk concretely, yet they allow us to be satisfied answering some "whys" with nothing more than "something there is."

I look forward to the wall-accepters now, though my heart remains with the wall-rejecters. They both teach me. I learn.

As a teacher, I always try to "ask to know what I was walling in, or walling out," and get students to do that too. Misunderstandings leave "our fingers rough with handling them" but also lead us to a clearer understanding of what we're doing or not doing. The more we think we know what we're teaching, the more we're shown our misconceptions and prejudices. That is how our teaching souls are revealed. Some walls come down, and better ones go up, and we see ourselves on both sides.

Surgery and Cranes

Early in my teaching career in Japan, I stood in front of my class to deliver some upsetting news. Standing at the podium, I looked out at my intensive English class. They were good students, many of them had lived abroad, and they were motivated and switched on. They could tell something was up by my frown and formality.

"I'll be gone next week. So, another teacher will take over the next five classes. You have a paper due, and you need to finish the new reading and be ready to discuss it when I return next Wednesday."

"Why are you missing class, sensei?" one student asked.

"I have to have some surgery." A deep hush. "But it's not serious." Deeper hush.

"What kind of surgery?"

This was my first full-time university job, and I had worked hard to teach students to ask questions about the details and the big picture in every class. I required them to write down fifteen questions on every article and showed them how to use those questions actively to engage with the text and with each other. Now, that technique was coming home to roost. I would miss a week from the intensive class, which required a lot of regular work, and I needed to explain about the substitute teacher and assignments.

"It's an outpatient surgery in America, a small thing, but in Japan, they want you to rest before returning to work."

"If it's small, why do you need a week to recover?" another student asked.

"That sounds serious," someone added.

"Where is it?" another asked.

All eyes were on me. I took a breath, realizing that many of them had parents, friends, relatives, and even themselves with health issues. And they were not naive. They were a great class.

"It's my right testicle. It's a common procedure like a vasectomy." Needless to say, I usually don't mention my balls in public. They remain hidden under layers of clothing and are rarely spoken of as propriety demands. Still, I'd maybe lost my students with the vocabulary, something I'd taught them to work around by restating complicated sentences, phrases, or words in simpler terms.

Though I'd taught them not to translate back and forth, I went for Japanese. The other option was pointing. "*Kogan*." The medical word for testicle drew a couple of frowns, and one girl leaned over for a translation from the girl beside her. She looked surprised. "*Kintama*," I said, using the more common term, which translates more like "balls."

It took them a minute to process that, as it had taken me a couple of painful months to process it myself. I'd been knocked into a cycle of pain with a hydrocele, which swelled up and got infected. Antibiotics helped, but it recurred and swelled right back up again.

"Are you going to be all right?" one girl asked.

"I'm going to be fine." I knew they'd heard a lifetime of excuses from authority figures, but they let that one go. I ended class with admonitions to study hard with the new teacher. The bell rang, and they lingered, gathering their things. They clicked out of student mode and came up to wish me well before trickling into the hallway, unsure whether to act cheerful or worried. I wasn't sure how to act myself. I helped them translate "*O-daiji-ni*" to "Get well soon."

I reached up to wipe off the chalkboard and felt another shot of pain. For a couple of weeks, a wrong step, mounting my bike, or even rolling over on the couch hurt so badly that it took my breath away. That was nothing compared to having the hydrocele drained with a large needle and what looked like a turkey baster. The first time I had it drained, even the nurse looked away. When a nurse winces, you know it'll be bad. It was.

After the third draining, the doctor said it was better to have it removed, a procedure, he claimed, was not much different from a vasectomy. A bigger section of the tube would be cut out. Telling my wife about the surgery was bad, but telling the students was worse.

You never notice your balls much of the day. A scratch, a juggle, a reset, and, of course, the pleasure they can deliver during sex, but usually, they rest quietly in what one underwear company called "a ballpark pouch." Mine didn't rest. A physical had turned up the hydrocele a few years before. The doctor was fascinated as she had never seen one before. She flashed a light on my scrotum, everything flopping around, and explained that it wasn't a big deal unless it hurt. I let it go. Two years later, it hurt.

Essentially, it was like a third ball that had formed from a twist in the vas deferens, the coiled tube that carries sperm from the epididymis through the prostate, where seminal fluid is added, and finally, finally through the penis and out the urethra. It's an amazing little system. When it works. When it gets twisted like a garden hose, it balloons up with the pressure and hurts like any pain simile you care to mention.

Surgery or even a minor health problem in another language and another country requires double the energy. There's the language, first of all, though my doctors spoke enough English to explain the basics. The main surgeon didn't speak much English, but he knew all the medical vocabulary, so I pieced those together with my Japanese. The anesthesiologist had lived in the States, and his fluency in English relaxed me. But your body makes the most sense in your native language, and even then, the words slip from their referent parts.

There were Japanese rules about bandages, food, excretion, and sleep. Filling in forms in Japanese isn't easy. The gown was too small. They wanted me to wear a kind of loincloth, but I stuck with cotton undies. People were different too. In my room, there was a young man in his teens whose family was always there, chatty and friendly. In one of the other beds lay a sullen and withdrawn salaryman whose wife dutifully brought tea, snacks, clean clothes, and no conversation. My wife visited, but when she left, I was the only foreigner.

The day before the surgery, a nurse explained she needed to prep me for the surgery, which meant shaving me from my belly button to my knees. When I pulled my gown aside, she and another nurse looked at more hair than the usual Japanese patient. They set to work, a delicate matter. The razor looked cheaper than I would have liked, but I trusted her, concerned only when she talked about her salary being lower than she wanted. When razors are near your delicate areas, you want people paid well.

A group of medical students crowded in to see the specimen I presented. They nodded thoughtfully as the teacher explained how hydroceles are in the textbooks.

They walked to the next learning specimen, and I pulled up my pants and went back to reading. I'd packed a copy of Moby Dick to read in the hospital. At least my balls would not be harpooned on the high seas! Just a scalpel wielded by a trained hand.

My wife and I met with the surgeon and two of his team the night before the surgery. It went smoothly until he mentioned getting the sliced-out tissues examined for cancerous growth. I hadn't thought of that. It would take two weeks to get the results back. The shock of that possibility added to the culture shock and the general pre-surgery nerves, but I tried to make light of it. Joking's always been my best defense mechanism. I told my wife this was an unavoidable chapter in culture shock—surgery in a foreign country. My wife's defense mechanism is to remain silent, though, so she went home quietly, promising to visit the next day after the surgery.

I declined full anesthesia and took the local from the stomach down. "Like childbirth," the anesthesiologist joked in English. I tried to talk as much as I could, but with the anesthetics kicking in, I felt underwater. What a pleasant ride to the Japanese operating room. As they adjusted the lights and prepped their tools and my fragile body, I told them how much the room looked like the shows on TV. They nodded and smiled beneath their masks. They strung up a small drape to block my view of the proceedings and got to work.

After a short time, the surgeon plucked up a bit of tissue in his forceps. "*Sensei, mite kudasai. Kore dake desu.* Professor, please look at. It's just this." He'd started calling me "sensei" after I told him I was a teacher. I hoped it would make him more careful or more respectful. Looking at the snipped-out bit, I mumbled, "*Sodai gomi.*" Everyone in the operating room laughed. *Sodai gomi* is the term for "large-size trash," a special category in the complex recycling system of Tokyo for which you have to arrange pick-up and pay an extra disposal fee.

For the record, it's not easy to get a roomful of medical professionals to laugh in another language when your scrotum is cut open on an operating table. My wife has never believed I actually said that, but I did. It's maybe the pinnacle of my language learning accomplishments, a second-language speech contest if ever there was one.

In recovery, I waited for my digestive tract to start working again. I recorded my urine output and let the nurses stethoscope my belly for sounds of peristaltic motion. I was curious about the stitches but didn't have the nerve to look just yet. I thanked the nurses, filled in the last few forms, paid the bill, and walked to the taxi stand.

When I finally got down to disinfecting and re-bandaging the repair scene a couple of days later, I marveled at the short, single cut and the tight, neat stitchwork. I hobbled around the house for a couple of days, playing out my victimhood with diminishing sympathy from my wife, eating comfort food, and finishing Moby Dick. I still had a couple of chapters to go.

When Monday's return to classes rolled around, I prepared what I'd say to the students in the first class back. I had a handful of jokes I would pack into a speech about the brevity of life, the importance of learning, and the value of knowing the limits of the mind and body. I wanted to turn my experience into learning for the students and—as all teachers know—learning for myself. I wanted to explain how all experiences, especially with pain and fear, reveal lessons about life. I was a teacher not just of the English language, but of the world's big themes.

Walking across campus, the sun seemed brighter than I remembered, the trees greener, and the campus livelier. I knew it hadn't changed. I had. In my office, I gathered the textbook, roll sheet, and materials, thinking more about what to say. Colleagues poked their heads in my office door to welcome me back with various ribald comments. After joking, though, the male colleagues invariably winced or shuddered. But whatever the reaction, it was nice to redirect the Achilles' heel aspect of testicles toward the bawdy, slapstick side. I heard testicle jokes for a year thereafter.

I carried my bag across the green and into the main teaching building, taking the stairs to the second floor gingerly. I wouldn't be sitting down and getting up too often during class discussions for a while. And did I notice a glance or two from other students as I passed? Perhaps they gossiped, but I wasn't that worried. It was over, after all. I took a breath and stepped into the classroom, ready to deliver my big speech.

As I walked to the podium, the students stood and applauded. That stopped me in my tracks. Tears sprang to my eyes, and chills covered my back. I looked at them and, not knowing what else to do, bowed.

Two students came forward with a thick bunch of long strings of folded, colored paper. I didn't know what it was at first, but after they draped it over my lesson plans, I realized it was *senbazuru*, a thousand origami cranes they folded for me while I was gone. The rainbow of bright colors and crisp folds must have taken the whole week. They strung them together as neatly as my stitches.

I forgot about my speech. They applauded again and handed me a Western-style get-well-soon card with all their names.

The traditional Japanese symbol of good wishes for longevity, peace, and health came from a story about a Hiroshima survivor who folded several hundred paper cranes before succumbing to radiation poisoning. When she died, her classmates finished the rest of the one thousand. Since then, every year in Hiroshima and other temples across Tokyo and around the world, a thousand cranes are folded as prayer, offering, and condolence. I had my own.

Pulled and stretched in so many directions as I was, overpowered by fear about my body and my gratitude for the students I had, somehow the cranes did the trick. My stitches healed up nicely and didn't even hurt when the surgeon pulled them out. The test for cancer came back negative, and I was back biking and striding upstairs in a couple of weeks.

I've never mentioned my testicles in class again—never needed to, thankfully—and I've lost the card they gave me, but I've kept the cranes dangling from one wall or another ever since. I want to remember what my students taught me. They taught me more than I'd ever be able to teach them. Looking back on it, the student's cranes might be why I've stayed in Japan ever since.

Glossary

anzu—apricot

backu shimasu—backing up

bonenkai—end of the year party held in December

butoh—a form of modern Japanese dance, usually with white paint on the dancers

Chidorigafuchi—park in central Tokyo famed for its moat and cherry trees, near the Imperial Palace

Edo—the former name for Tokyo

Fujimi—a place from where Mount Fuji can be seen

ganbatte—go for it, keep going, good luck

gogatsubyo—literally May disease, term for the depressed feeling in May after the liveliness of April

gomi—trash

goshugi—gift money given, usually at a Japanese wedding

gyoen—park

Hakone—an area outside Tokyo famed for *onsen* and beautiful views of nature

hanami—literally, flowing viewing, but anytime viewing flowers, usually cherry trees

heri—silk border at the edge of tatami mats

hikidemono—return gift given at a wedding

igusa—the particular rush plant used for tatami

Irrashaimase—Welcome!

Itadakimasu—to humbly receive, usually said it the beginning of a meal to show gratitude

izakaya—Japanese style pub

jin—people, often added on to another word like "America-jin"

jirei—the official appointment of employment or to a new position

kadomatsu—literally, gate pine, a decoration put in front of doors and entryways at New Year

kanji—the Chinese characters

kanpai—literally drain the glass, or cheers, said when drinking or toasting

kintama—balls or testicles

kissaten—coffee shop or tearoom

koan—a paradox or riddle given to students of Zen Buddhism to avoid logic and apprehend directly

kogan—testicles

kotowaza—Japanese proverb

Manyoshu—the oldest collection of Japanese tanka poetry, often thought of as the start of Japanese culture

mawari no hitotachi—the surrounding people, a constant concern in Japanese society

meishi—name cards

mikoshi—a portable shrine carried on the shoulders during festivals

mingei—folk craft or folk art

Musashino—area in western Tokyo

nijikai—after party

nomikai—drinking party

o-daiji-ni—Get well soon

ochugen—gifts given in summer to maintain relationship or offer thanks

Ogikubo—station name and area in western Tokyo along the Chuo Line

Omotesando—swank area in central Tokyo with chic boutiques and shops

onsen—hot springs

onshi—honored teacher, formal term for one's former teacher

osechi—traditional Japanese New Year food, usually made in advance, or nowadays, bought

oseibo—gifts given in summer to maintain relationship or offer thanks

oshibori—the towel given to clean one's hands before a meal

osoji—literally big cleaning, usually a big clean of one's home or office at New Year

sakura—cherry blossoms

seiza—sitting position with one's knees folded under

senbazuru—a thousand cranes, folded paper cranes as a symbol of hope or healing

sensei—teacher, doctor, professor, a respectful term

shakaijin—literally society person, term referring to a member of society, usually working, not a student

shikari—the preparation time before a sumo match starts

shitashiki naka nimo reigi ari—even among friends, there is courtesy, a Japanese saying

sodai gomi—big trash, collected on a special day requiring an additional fee.

sudare—slatted blinds covering windows or doors

sugoi—amazing, incredible, fantastic

Takumen—an online site that delivers frozen ramen

Tanabata Festival—a summer festival, also called the star festival, on the 7th day of the 7th month celebrating the meeting of two celestial lovers

tatami—mats made for flooring

tatemae—the external, polite mask to avoid confrontation, different from *honne*, one's true feeling

Toshiro Mifune—famous Japanese actor, who often played samurai characters.

Ueno—an area in northeast Tokyo famed for a large park, museums, and market

ume—plum

ushigaeru—toad

washitsu—Japanese style room, usually with tatami

yoshitsu—western style room

Thanks

Thanks to Publications

The following articles were originally published in other magazines. I am grateful to those editors and magazines for their encouragement and support of my writing.

"Rights in the Matter." The Font, 2018, Vol.1, http://thefontjournal.com/creative-non-fiction-2018-vol-1/. (ISSN 2203-4412).

"The Language Dance," The Font, 2020, Vol.2, http://thefontjournal.com/current-issue-8/. (ISSN 2203-4412).

"Context for My Outrage," The Font, 2020, Vol.1, http://thefontjournal.com/current-issue-8/. (ISSN 2203-4412).

"Train Time" White Enzo Issue 5, 2021, http://www.whiteenso.com/issue-5-table-of-contents.html.

"Tokyo Masked." Courrier Japon クーリエ・ジャポン, December 28, 2021. ウイルスは東京の魅力を奪っていった」 https://courrier.jp/news/archives/272785/

"Before I Taught a Poem I'd Ask to Know." The Font 2022, Vol.1, https://thefontjournal.com/before-i-taught-a-poem-id-ask-to-know/. (ISSN 2203-4412).

"Turnabout is Fair Play—Wedding Speech," The Font 2023 Vol. 1, https://thefontjournal.com/current-issue-2023-vol-1/. (ISSN 2203-4412).

"Beauty Blossoming—Tokyo's Cherry Trees." Musubi Kiln 29 March 2024. https://musubikiln.com/blogs/column/beauty-blossoming-japan-s-cherry-trees.

"A Procession of Pottery: Onsen in Hakone." Musubi Kiln 15 January 2024. https://musubikiln.com/blogs/column/a-procession-of-pottery-onsen-in-hakone.

"Outside the Classroom." The Font, 2024 Spring. https://thefontjournal.com/outside-the-classroom/. (ISSN 2203-4412).

Thanks to People

For my students, who always seem to understand on the last day of class when I share Mark Twain's admonition: "Don't let your schooling get in the way of your education." For my chums, who taught me not to be over-confident. Some came to Tokyo. Some haven't. Yet.

> They taught me not to be so nice
> The way I tipped my hat.
> And when I slipped upon the ice,
> They saw that I fell more than twice.
> I'm grateful for that.
> "The Chums" by Theodore Roethke

And as always, for my wife, who listened to the first spoken musings, read the first written drafts, and put up with me all the while. "I'll stick with you, baby, 'til the money runs out."

About the author

Days, I work as a professor of American Literature at Meiji Gakuin University. My students' questions and responses to American novels, films, poetry, art, and music keep me on my cultural toes. Faculty meetings, I could do without. But it's been a good working home.

I have written for many publications: Newsweek Japan for a decade, The Japan Times for a dozen years, a bilingual jazz magazine called Jazznin, and Artscape Japan, among others.

I also run my own website about the jazz scene in Tokyo, Jazz in Japan, at: www.jazzinjapan.com.

And I have an award-winning detective series set in Tokyo. Detective Hiroshi, the lead in the novels, has his own view of Tokyo. Check them out at:

www.michaelpronko.com.

Most of these essays were posted on my website or were published with journals and magazines, but some are here for the first time. All of them were rewritten for this collection.

I was born and raised in Kansas City, so people always ask how I ended up in Tokyo. There are plenty of reasons to go to Tokyo, but the number of reasons to stay are perhaps fewer. Most of those reasons are evident in the writing here.

I studied philosophy at college, and though it might sound strange, I approach Tokyo with a philosophical attitude. Maybe that's a defense, but with that approach in mind, the interesting sides of the city open up. In any event, this is the fourth non-fiction book I've written about Tokyo, plus seven in the detective series, and I still feel like there's a lot more to say.

As I struggle those things into words, I'll keep teaching at Meiji Gakuin, living in western Tokyo, going out for jazz, and writing about Tokyo.

www.ingramcontent.com/pod-product-compliance
Lightning Source LLC
Chambersburg PA
CBHW030517080526
44586CB00011B/227